THE D

THAT

THE DIFFERENCE THAT DISABILITY MAKES

Rod Michalko

Temple University Press
PHILADELPHIA

Temple University Press, Philadelphia 19122
Copyright © 2002 by Temple University
All rights reserved
Published 2002
Printed in the United States of America

⊖ The paper used in this publication meets the requirements of the American National
Standard for Information Sciences—Permanence of Paper for Printed Library Materials,
ANSI Z39.48-1984

Library of Congress Cataloging-in-Publication Data

Michalko, Rod
  The difference that disability makes / Rod Michalko.
    p. cm.
  Includes bibliographical references and index.
  ISBN 1-56639-933-5 (cloth : alk. paper) — ISBN 1-56639-934-3 (pbk. : alk. paper)
    1. Sociology of disability.   2. Handicapped—Psychology.   3. Handicapped—
Attitude.   I. Title.

HV1568.M53 2002
305.9′0816—dc21

                                                                2001046308

For Smokie

Contents

Acknowledgments   ix

1   Introduction   1

2   Home Is Where the Heart Is   17

3   The Social Location of Suffering   41

4   Coming Face-to-Face with Suffering   73

5   The Birth of Disability   113

6   Image and Imitation   143

     Notes   177

     References   181

     Index   189

Acknowledgments

Rarely, if ever, is a book written alone, and there are many to whom I owe thanks. Much of the writing of this book has been supported by a grant from the Social Sciences and Humanities Research Council of Canada. I am indebted to Frances Baker for word processing; she typed my dictation and did so with speed, skill, and patience. I am grateful to Debbie Murphy, who assisted me greatly in photocopying and printing.

I am especially grateful to Dan MacInnis, Robert Kennedy, and Will Sweet for their assistance with Latin phrases. Dan MacInnis spent time giving me many insights into ideas and practices of normalcy, and for this, I am grateful. I am also indebted to Dan Ahern, who generously shared with me his thoughts and work on the phenomenon of suffering. Over the past year, I had the privilege of supervising the honors thesis work of Lindsay McVicar. Her work involved theorizing the body, and our initial supervisory relationship soon turned into one of collaboration. Lindsay kindly offered her time and energy to read, edit, and comment on my work. I am also indebted to Terri Pitts for her careful and patient reading of the page proofs. As always, Janet Francendese provided me with much encouragement, and I still marvel at her skill of shepherding a book through the often tedious publication process. I am very grateful to Debby Smith for her impeccable copy editing. She allowed the spirit of my book to shine through its pages a little more brightly. David Mitchell and Christopher Doran not only provided insights on this work but also gave me suggestions for my next book. I am especially indebted to those disabled people who so generously gave of their time to tell their stories.

I am most indebted to my partner and colleague, Tanya Titchkosky. While I am solely responsible for what appears in the following pages, this book would have been impossible without the ongoing collaboration I am so fortunate to share with Tanya.

Finally, I owe a debt of thanks to my guide dog, Smokie. He guided me through our world, and he pointed me to ever deeper understandings of blindness. On June 4, 2001, Smokie died. This work is dedicated to him.

THE DIFFERENCE
THAT DISABILITY MAKES

1

Introduction

isability and suffering have been paired throughout history and remain inseparable companions to this day (Stiker 1999). Suffering always defines a disabled person as a type: one who suffers an affliction, who suffers punishment for some wrongdoing; one who is forced to bear the weight of divine intervention, who is barred from the center of society and relegated to its margins. Contemporary culture, particularly Western culture since the Industrial Revolution, represents disability as something that should be prevented or cured and sees disability as a tragedy that befalls some people. No one aspires to be that type, a disabled person.

Being a person who is not welcome, who is feared, pitied, and looked upon as a type no one would aspire to be is often difficult to bear, as I was reminded on a recent trip to Toronto. Toronto is a cosmopolitan city with a highly diverse population. But this modern and admired feature contributed to the disturbing character of my experience.

My partner, Tanya Titchkosky, and I moved from Toronto several years ago. Since then we have been living in Antigonish, Nova Scotia, and teaching sociology at Saint Francis Xavier University. Antigonish is a small town and we began to miss the big city and our friends there. Our respective and collaborative research projects also made it necessary to visit Toronto. It was time to go to the big city for a couple of weeks.

Everything went smoothly for the first while. Our friends Kate and Mark picked us up from the airport and drove us to the University of Toronto residence where we had arranged to stay during our visit. But the room proved to be inappropriate for our needs. It was on the top floor of an old and very beautiful three-story building. In keeping with the architecture, the first three flights of stairs were very wide and of a smooth stone construction with banisters that did not run the entire length of the stairs. Beyond these three flights was a very narrow, very long and somewhat rickety flight of wooden stairs that spilled out into the corridor that led to our room. This last flight of stairs was also equipped with a banister but only on the right ascending side and only partway up.

Tanya and her dog, Cassis, followed me and my guide dog, Smokie, as we entered the building and, key in hand, made our way to the stairs. Smokie, responding to my request, found the stairs and stopped to let me know where they were. I located the first stair, gripped the heavy suitcase in my right hand and, flexing the fingers of my left around Smokie's harness, said, "Forward, Smoke."

Despite some slipping and sliding that Smokie experienced on the smooth stone of the first three flights of stairs and my having to careen the suitcase up the last flight of wooden stairs, we reached our room. It was very small with barely enough room for the four of us to turn around. It was also quite hot and stuffy and the one tiny window did not promise much relief. After giving Smokie and Cassis some much needed water, Tanya and I sat on the edge of the bed and wondered how we were going to manage for the next two weeks. Still, we were back in Toronto and happy to be there, and so we decided to think about our situation later and for now take Smokie and Cassis into the courtyard, where they could run around a little and relieve themselves after their long plane ride and trip from the airport.

We left our room and, once more, I asked Smokie to find the stairs. He did so and let me know by stopping. I said, "Forward," and as Smokie began to guide me down the stairs, I reached out with my right hand to find the banister. Nothing but a wall met my reach. Without a banister, I had to pull back on Smokie's harness to counter his pull down the stairs so that we would not proceed too rapidly. Then, the last three flights of stairs. Again, Smokie found them and stopped. Again, no banister. After two or three steps, however, my hand inadvertently hit one. Grasping it, I lessened my pull on Smokie's harness and allowed him to guide me down the stairs at his customary quick pace. Suddenly, no banister but the stairs continued. Smokie and I took the last three or four stairs at a pace a little quicker than safety dictated. Nevertheless, we adjusted and made our way more slowly down the remaining stairs and out into the courtyard. Tanya and I unharnessed our dogs and let them roam the grassy and treed area of the courtyard.

We were happy for Smokie and Cassis and we both laughed as Tanya described the excitement and thoroughness with which our dogs investigated their new environment. Even though Tanya had trained Cassis to do guide dog work and she would be working Cassis in harness for our stay in Toronto, Tanya is not blind. She acquired Cassis about six months after I arrived home with Smokie from the guide dog training school. Driven by interest and curiosity and perhaps even empathy, Tanya began training Cassis to guide while she was still a puppy. Because of Tanya's training and, I suspect, Smokie's example, by the time Cassis was a year old, she was a very competent guide dog.

We were now back in Toronto, where Smokie and I had spent our first five years together and where Cassis and Tanya had learned to feign both guide dog work and blindness. Their feigning a guide dog team has allowed Tanya, Cassis, Smokie, and me to enter public establishments that bar all pets except working dogs. And it has had the added, serendipitous benefit of enhancing our research in Disability Studies. Even though research was not part of the motivation for training Cassis to do guide dog work, both the training and the subsequent work have given Tanya and me an entrée into the rich and fertile realm of social interaction that occurs in the meeting of blind and sighted persons in public places.

With the dogs' peeing and sniffing over with, we harnessed them up and set out for our room. This time, despite the lack of suitcases, the trip up the stairs was not much easier. We still had to contend with the slippery stone stairs, the narrow wooden ones, and, of course, those ineffectual banisters.

And the room was hotter than before. Smokie and Cassis dealt with the heat by drinking more water and finding comfortable places to lie down on the floor. Tanya and I resumed our seats on the bed, since it was the only place to sit, and became more serious about the situation. We soon agreed that we could not manage several trips a day up and down these stairs over the next two weeks. We made our decision. Tanya grabbed the telephone book and I the telephone and she began reading telephone numbers of downtown Toronto hotels to me. It took about two hours, but eventually we found a spacious, air-conditioned suite of rooms in a downtown apartment hotel with a wonderful adjacent park for Smokie and Cassis. Our two weeks' stay in Toronto was both comfortable and productive.

The incident that jolted me into remembering the type I am came during the two-hour marathon on the telephone. We had difficulty finding a hotel because we needed one downtown for a specific two weeks. Most of the hotels we called had vacancies only for part of the time, others did not have any convenient relief areas for the dogs, and still others were far beyond our budget. After about an hour, when Tanya and I were beginning to feel desperate, I found a hotel with two-week vacancies. "Great," I said into the telephone. "Let me tell you our situation. I'm a blind person with . . ." Before I could finish, the person on the other end of the telephone line said, emphatically, "We don't rent rooms to blind people." I was in Toronto. This was my home for several years. I was in a big cosmopolitan city with a rich cultural and ethnic diversity. It was 1999. All these thoughts flashed through my mind as I digested the words that had just spilled from the telephone. The only word I could speak in response was, "Pardon?" Again I heard, "We don't rent rooms to blind people." And I said that that is against the law and that I was going to call the police. The person said, "Go ahead" and hung up. In disbelief, I slowly returned the receiver to its cradle and turned to Tanya who, by this time, was asking what was wrong. I told her and we both sat quietly for a few moments. Finally, Tanya broke the silence. "Shit! I'm sorry," she said.

Who Am I?

"Who am I?" is a question, according to Hannah Arendt (1958), that we ask and answer every time we speak and every time we act. Our identities are couched in speech and action and we speak and act with and from them. In a social world, others use our identity to define us and we use it to define ourselves. These identities are "ready-made" for us to step into as we immerse ourselves in the social world (Taylor 1989, 25–35).

In this book I interrogate the process of identity formation and the social and political significance of our stepping into our identities. While our identities are ready-made and we do step into them, as Taylor suggests, they are nonetheless *made* and are not natural. The ready-made aspect of identity results in our seeing ourselves and being seen by others as types. The types that define us can be sources of enjoyment or suffering.

There are many conventionally recognizable types that encompass the concept of social identity. They fall into categories of race, gender, ethnicity, profession, and so on. Now another type has been added to this list—disabled. Disability has existed as long as human life has existed but only recently has figured in human identity. It has generally been conceived of as something that happens to a person and thus as not a natural part of the human condition. Depending upon the culture in which it occurs (Ingstad and Whyte 1995), disability has been conceived of as being brought on by disease, accident, or flawed genes or curses and other supernatural phenomena, or it is retribution for wrongdoing often going back generations. Disability is natural only insofar as it is seen as the accident of nature or the intention of the supernatural. Still, it was understood as an "attachment," as something extra that, for whatever reason, happened to a person.

Traditionally, disability has been understood as a phenomenon that has a tremendous effect (usually a negative one) on a person's life but is not related to identity, to whom a person *essentially is*. Thus, disability is interpreted as happenstance and disabled persons are viewed, and view themselves, as persons *with* disabilities or as persons *first*. In fact, the sociological concept of "master-status" is often invoked to characterize the negativity of seeing disability as an essential aspect of one's identity.

Recent developments in the disability movement and in Disability Studies, however, have offered an alternative, if not competing, dimension to what has remained to this day the dominant perspective. Disability can now be understood from the perspective of politics. It is more than merely a private happenstance that must be suffered in the realm of privacy; it is also a public matter that must be suffered in and through the polis. Disability is not an exclusively individual issue; it is a collective one.

Nevertheless, those of us who are disabled find ourselves in the midst of many different ideas about disability. Regardless of how disability is conceived, we live our lives in these conceptions. Since every collective has ways of understanding and representing it, disability is lived in the midst of these collective representations and, therefore, bears a social and political character.

The idea that disability is a collective issue, however, is not easy to grasp. It seems to run counter to the traditional Western social and political philosophies, influenced by the Enlightenment, that place a tremendous importance on the individual. Combine this emphasis with belief in the superiority of reason and mind over the passions and vicissitudes of the body, also a legacy of the Enlightenment, and we can begin to understand why disability has long been conceived of as only an individual issue.

In keeping with this traditional concept of disability as an individual issue, society sees its responsibility to disability in the provision of preventive, curative, and rehabilitative measures. Disability must be prevented; failing this, it must be cured; if it can be neither prevented nor cured, society must see that the person is rehabilitated, the "final solution." These responses are in keeping with the biomedical version of what it means to be human. This version, which emphasizes adjustment and adaptation, plays a dominant role in the contemporary understanding of disability. Unfortunate as it is, disability is something that *happens* to some of us and it is up to us to take advantage of what society gives us in the form of medical and rehabilitation programs—and adjust.

The reasonableness and simplicity of this traditional perspective makes it quite attractive. Seeing disability as originating anywhere else than in accident and biology raises other questions about why, and these questions, because they are metaphysical, are often thought of as better left alone. It is better to leave questions of identity alone, too, to avoid having to address the question, "Who am I now that I am disabled?" The biomedical model provides an easy and attractive answer to this question: "You are who you always were. You haven't changed. You remain an individual, a person *with* a disability." Identity firmly in hand in the form of "person-first" ideology, a disabled person can now make his or her way through the social and physical world with its labyrinth of obstacles, such as hotels that refuse to rent rooms and negative attitudes that translate into sympathetic pats on the back. Ironically, this sort of "making" reproduces and reinforces the dominant ideology that one is a person first.

I understood my experience as a blind person in this way for many years. In fact, this understanding has not entirely left me and, despite my efforts to shove it aside, it makes an appearance from time to time. I try to keep in mind Friedrich Nietzsche's observation (1967, 493) that "what does not destroy us makes us stronger." I began experiencing sight loss in late childhood and I did have some sense that it might just kill me.

> I lay there on my bed crying a little, but only a little, which surprised me because I was quite worried. I couldn't see the blackboard for the last couple of days now. But today, was really tough. A line-drive was hit right to me and I saw it and then I didn't see it! It hit me right on the cheek. That had never happened before. I couldn't believe it—I saw it then I didn't see it. Laying there I didn't know what was wrong. Remember, I was only nine years old.
> I could hear my mother and my grandmother talking in the kitchen. They were speaking their first language but I could understand them. My grandmother said she was getting old and that she couldn't hear well any more nor could she see well. She said that soon she would die. My body froze in fright. I thought, I really thought, that I was dying. What else could it be? It seems silly now, but I spent the next few days testing my hearing to make sure that it was holding up. (Michalko 1998, 36)

That sight loss represented premature aging and death was beyond question for me at this point. That it would make me stronger, however, was certainly doubtful. I just wanted this fuzzy and unclear world to go away. Playing baseball, reading blackboards and books, just playing—that is what I wanted. I did not want a life without these things and, what is more, I could not even imagine such a life. But more than anything, I did not want to die, not yet anyway.

Over the next two or three years, I was examined by several ophthalmologists. But even after the first of these examinations, the verdict was in: I was blind. This struck me as odd at the time. After all, I could see. Perhaps line drives were disappearing, but I could see. The ophthalmologist explained this oddity to my parents, who then tried to explain it to me. My macula had developed pigmentation, probably genetically based, causing my visual acuity to decline and the sharpness of the images my eyes saw to deteriorate. It was like a broken fine-tuning switch on a television, my parents explained. Because I could not recognize the "big E" on an eye chart, I was "legally blind." All of the ophthalmologists I saw at that time said that I would retain this "10 percent vision" for most of my life and that I might lose all of my sight but not until well into adulthood.

So I was not dying after all. I could still play some sports, especially those involving a ball bigger than a baseball, such as football. Reading would have to be done holding the book a little closer to my eyes and sitting a little closer to the blackboard. Losing all of my sight would not come until late adulthood and, from my point of view at age eleven or twelve, that was forever and knowing that I might lose my eyesight at that time seemed as abstract to me as knowing that I would die. So blindness continued to hold the same meaning for me as death did. I would eventually go blind and I would eventually die, same thing.

About a year after the line drive disappeared, we had moved to a large city because, my parents reasoned, we would surely find more sophisticated medical and educational services. But even "big city" ophthalmology could not loosen the grip that legal blindness had on me, and educational services had little to offer me. Mainstreaming had not yet caught on as an educational theory for disabled students, and the alternatives were stark in their opposition—it was either "blind school" several hundreds of miles away from home or regular school in my neighborhood.

Legal as my blindness was, neither my parents nor I thought of me as blind. After all, 10 percent was pretty good sight in the "country of the blind" (Wells 1911). Thus, the choice was plain from the beginning—I would attend regular school. The Department of Education had some large-print books, as well as some recordings of books, and occasionally a "special" teacher would visit me to help me out. With this minimal assistance and with the help of my parents, I finished the rest of my elementary education and completed junior high school.

High school was a turning point for me. We moved, not a great distance, but far enough that I would go to a different high school with students who had no idea that I was legally blind. Passing as fully sighted became my strongest desire and I went about it with a devastating single-mindedness (Michalko 1982, 1998, 102–27). I knew, on some level, that I had been trying to pass since the line drive hit me in the cheek, but now I was fully aware of it and relentlessly pursued the life of a sighted adolescent. I employed every interactional strategy possible to pass myself off as someone who was totally sighted. I could see, even if it was just a little, and I *was* sighted. That was *my self*, my identity, and even though blindness was creeping its way into me, I held it in abeyance on what I quickly came to experience as the interactional battlefield of passing. I now made conscious use of the taken-for-granted character of sight left over from my days as a fully sighted child. But the skill I cultivated most desperately was that of observation. I came to see sightedness as a culture with customs, folkways, and gestures—with its own language. That I did so was something I realized only later in life. Nonetheless, I imitated this culture to perfection. For all practical purposes (Garfinkel 1967), I was a high school student who was sighted.

But my identity as a sighted adolescent went far beyond its interactional accomplishment. Regardless of any legal definition, I was not blind; I was sighted; that was me. My passing was motivated by the adolescent desire for normalcy, by the desire to be "one of the guys." But there was more to it than that: I wanted to be me, my sighted self.

Blindness continued to threaten this sighted self, which I clung to as tightly as I could, constantly battling the blindness that was slowly entering me. I could still see and no matter how little, that was the "I" I was and for which I fought. Sightedness and blindness could not co-habit my identity. I was one or the other but not both. One of them would have to die and I was doing my best to kill blindness before it killed me.

I was as certain that I would "go blind" as I was that I would die. But blindness was far closer to me than death. My life as "one of the guys" was what blindness threatened. Once blindness took over my self, it would destroy any semblance of normalcy I had. Passing allowed me to keep blindness a secret from all other students in the high school. And it allowed me to keep blindness a secret from me as well. My passing was truly an act of repression.

Disability, Lennard Davis (1997, 1) writes, is "always an actively repressed *memento mori* for the fate of the normal body." Steeped as it is in the biomedical understanding of the human body, disability reminds us of the body's fate, that the body is "normal" only temporarily. First the sight goes, then the hearing, then the rest of the body. Our sense of normalcy weakens in the remembrance of our fate. But the "normal body" is only the beginning of normalcy. Seeing line drives and black-boards, reading books, making eye contact all spring, or so we think, from the sense of our bodies as normal. The normal stuff of everyday life is threatened when our bodies lose a sense of their normalcy. Thus, disability also actively represses the fate of everyday life. Passing, then, is an act of repression because the presence of disability in everyday life reminds us of the fragile character of social interaction and threatens its existence (Goffman 1963).

It is small wonder that many of us who are disabled subscribe to the "person-first" ideology. We place the common ground of personhood before the not-so-common one of disability. Choosing personhood over disability emphasizes both the strength of personhood and its separation from the body. As much as we want to repress any memory of the fate of our bodies, we also want to be reminded of just how strong personhood is in the face of this fate. Disability can be our reminder. For disabled people, interaction with a nondisabled person is often a struggle to present the self (Goffman 1959) as *person* as the primary actor in this interaction and to disavow the "deviant" character of disability (Davis 1961). But suggesting that disability is merely a secondary feature of one's identity and that we are persons *first* and persons *with* disabilities disavows both deviance and disability. It refocuses attention from the disability to the person who happens to have it. For example, a few days after the hotel clerk told me that the hotel did not rent rooms to blind people, Tanya and I had dinner with friends and I told them about this incident. They were, of course, surprised that such a thing could happen in Toronto and asked whether I was thinking of legal action. During our discussion, one of our friends said, "And he didn't even know you." What she was implying was that the hotel clerk rejected not me but blindness. The clerk did not know the person behind the blindness; blindness came before the person. If blindness were put in its "proper place," our interaction would have been person-to-person rather than person-to-blindness. And so, my friend thought, if our interaction had been face-to-face rather than on the telephone, the clerk might have "seen" that I was indeed a person first and was in control of any of the negative aspects of blindness.

We often reason that interaction between disabled persons and nondisabled ones would diminish the fear of disability and the negative attitudes the nondisabled persons might harbor about it. Such interaction could change the thinking of nondisabled persons who imagine life with a disability only in negative terms. The hotel clerk, in my experience, responded to me on the basis of a version of blindness as an imagined life. Perhaps he could not imagine being blind in a hotel or perhaps a previous blind guest had set a room on fire and the clerk was stereotyping—if one blind person sets a room on fire, they'll all do it. Whatever the interpretation, the clerk's imagined life of blindness did not include hotel accommodation. I or, as my friend implied, my blindness was not welcome in his hotel.

This incident illustrates yet another feature of disability; not only does it repress our memory of the fate of the "normal body" but it also engenders a *memento vivere*, reminding us of the good fortune of a "normal life." Seeing a disabled person often evokes admiration, especially if the person is seen as overcoming his or her disability. This admiration is often extended to the most basic accomplishments. I recently attended a university convocation where an address was delivered by a woman upon whom the university had just conferred an honorary doctoral degree. In her address, she said that one of her mentors was a blind man who is married and has a family and a job. Her comments were greeted with resounding applause. There was no applause for the fact that the blind man was a mentor. Conversely, disability can also remind others of their good fortune and generates such adages as, "There but for the grace of God go I."

The person-first ideology grows out of these collective representations of disability but has not been able to rid the collective of negative representations of disability. We are still feared, we are still applauded for simple accomplishments, we are still not the type of person anyone wants to be, and we are still not welcome. The image nondisabled others have of disability does not yet include any association with "the good life." Lauri Klobas (1988) suggests that the image of disability represented in film and television has not changed much since the inception of those forms of entertainment. In contrast, she shows how the images of race and gender have changed positively over the decades. She is disturbed but not puzzled by her finding, which she considers self-evident, a "fact of disabled life." The media continue to employ images of disability, she points out, as part of an effort to demonstrate all conceivable foibles of individual and collective life. But we are still not welcome. And this fact ought to be both disturbing and puzzling. Klobas should be more interested in why disability is so resistant to changes of image and why the media resists changing the image of disability.

Choosing Disability

The biomedical paradigm claims disability for itself and treats disability as the continuous struggle of the "normal body" with itself. What is considered normal about the body is a product of the measuring of human achievement (Davis 1995; Thomson 1997a). Normal hearing, normal seeing, normal walking are achieved when the conception of the "normal body" is evoked as a method for understanding the body that quits hearing or seeing or walking, or the body that simply quits (Canguilhem 1991).

The biomedical paradigm sees disability as something wrong with the biological body and thus constructs disability as a medical problem. In other aspects of life as well, according to this paradigm, disability is a metaphor for a problem. I encountered one in Toronto, where I heard a traffic report on a local radio station announcing that a "disabled streetcar" was holding up traffic on Queen Street. This disability resulted in a traffic problem. The same evocation of normalcy exists in this example as in the example of disability as a medical problem. Like the body, the streetcar is not doing what it normally does and thus is causing problems. The disabled streetcar now represents a technical problem and the mechanics take over. If they cannot fix it, the streetcar is removed from the street. Medical doctors likewise take over the problem of disability. If they cannot fix it, the disabled person may not be welcome on the streets.

No one is likely to choose disability according to this sense of the world. The biomedical paradigm represents the dominant way of understanding the body and of defining what is normal and what is abnormal, particularly in Western cultures. Still, many of us live disabilities. Our lives are influenced by the ways our culture represents disability. We are living examples of those representations.

Choosing or reclaiming disability (Linton 1998) begins with the attempt to understand the representations that our culture has ready-made for us and to grasp the relationship between them and our individual and collective identities. With Arthur Frank (1995, 27), we must recognize that "the body is not mute, but it is inarticulate; it does not use speech, yet begets it." The body says nothing and so we speak on its behalf. This speech is found in the various interpretations societies develop regarding the body, which include definitions of what is a "normal" body and what is a "disabled" body. Disability is an example of the speech that the inarticulate body begets. Choosing disability also involves resisting the formulation of disability as a medical problem.[1] This resistance within the disability movement and Disability Studies has resulted in alternative, and even competing, interpretations of disability. But more important, it has allowed disability to be seen as worthy of choice.

I believe that disability is indeed a choice. This sentiment may be discomforting or even nonsensical to those who treat disability as a medical problem, but to those of us who are disabled as well as those of us who are engaged in Disability Studies, this sentiment is essential. Any political struggle involving disability and any connection we make between identity and disability necessarily begins with a conception of disability as choice. Thus, I begin my argument with the assumption that disability finds its sensibility within the ways in which a collective conceives of what it means to be human and how it makes a place for the individual in what it socially organizes as a human community. Making a place for difference, including disability, is a feature of every culture and society and my aim is to interrogate this "making" in relation to disability. I do not begin by defining disability but instead, along the way, I allow its meaning to emerge as I work through the various conceptions of disability that exist in collective life. [2] Disability is not a static entity amenable to definition in the empirical sense; it is a "fluid and shifting set of conditions" (Shildrick and Price 1996, 93). My aim, therefore, is to use the shifting set of conditions of my life and my society to capture the meaning of disability. This is not a book based on personal experience, however, because my experience, and anyone else's experience for that matter, is embedded in a collective.

In *The Mystery of the Eye and the Shadow of Blindness* (Michalko 1998), I explore the meaning of blindness. Using the heuristic device of "stages," I show how we come to form understandings of our blindness within our culture and how we then live our lives in and through these understandings. I also show how the dialectic between sightedness and blindness acts as a primal site for the development of such understandings.

In my second book, *The Two in One: Walking with Smokie, Walking with Blindness* (1999), I make extensive use of my experience with my guide dog Smokie, uncovering the world that Smokie brings to me as he guides me through it to develop the idea of guide as teacher. I try to show how the relationship that Smokie and I have is a derivative of the one between nature and society. There are many interpretations of nature and of society and there are many interpretations of the relationship between the two, just as there are many interpretations of blindness; within this manyness a blind person lives his or her life.

In this book, building on the ideas I raise in my first two, I focus on disability as a political act that is suffered by both disabled people and nondisabled ones, albeit differently. Suffering here does not refer to the conventional sense of "suffering a disability" but refers instead to the suffering of the multitude of interpretations of disability, the political acts that culturally organize and define disability—the suffering of our society's choices made in regard to the meaning of disability. The animating question I use to understand disability in this way is that raised by Irving Zola (1982, 244): "Why [has] a society been created and perpetuated which has excluded so many of its members?" Disabled himself, Zola asked this question of his society almost twenty years ago with regard to its exclusion of its disabled members. He did not expect an answer. Instead, he meant to issue a challenge to his society and to its nondisabled members as well as to those of us who are disabled. It is relatively easy, suggests Zola, to ask questions about matters of accessibility and their costs but not so easy to ask why these questions are necessary in the first place.

Why are we excluded? This is the question I asked myself after hanging up from my telephone conversation with the hotel clerk. Why was I not welcome in his hotel? Why does my society, *still today*, exclude so many of its members? As personal as this question might seem, it is a social and political one. Exclusion, intentional or not, is a political act and, therefore, a choice. Zola's society, as well as my own, has chosen to exclude its disabled members. In this exclusion, society has decided to include disability in particular ways, which I interrogate throughout this book.

This book is about the decisive character of exclusion and inclusion. It is also about the version of disability that must be chosen in order to see exclusion as an oriented and thus political act. Seeing exclusion as a choice is possible only when disability is understood as a choice and as a life worth living. I attempt to trace out the path that leads to exclusion and I also try to find the one that allows us to pose Zola's question. I welcome all readers, disabled or not, to join me in this quest.

A final note: throughout this book I make extensive use of my own experience as a blind person. I also make use of the experiences of others, some of whom are disabled, some not. To protect the identity of these people I have altered their names as well as other features. I use their experiences to narrate the life of disability as it emerges in the midst of our society. Whatever disability can teach us about itself and our society originates in the stories I explore in the following pages.

2

Home Is Where the Heart Is

My neighbor Stewart and I were talking in my office at the university. He was on campus and dropped by to offer me a ride home. Dan MacInnes, a colleague, walked by and, noticing us, came into to my office to say hello. Stewart asked Dan whether he was going to Scotland, as he often did, for both research and pleasure, at the end of the university term. Then he added, "You must know Scotland by heart by now." "By heart is the only way to know a place," Dan replied.

I was intrigued with what Dan said, especially since it came in response to such a prosaic comment. The idea of knowing a place "by heart" provoked many thoughts and feelings in me. Dan is Scottish and our university is in Nova Scotia, literally New Scotland. The town of Antigonish and the university bear the mark of the homeland. A trip to Scotland is, for Dan, a trip home: it is where he belongs; it is where his heart is. There are many ways to know Scotland but Dan knows it as a place to which he belongs. He is not a tourist when he goes to Scotland.

Knowing a place by heart suggests that that particular place is home. Whenever we conceive of a place as home, we *feel* at home there and we know, "by heart," that the

17

place welcomes us. We know, by heart, that we belong in that place and that it belongs to us.

This orientation to place implies the expectation that places we know by heart make a place for us. We do not need to make a place for ourselves at home. Our homes already make a place for us and we step into these ready-made places (Taylor 1989), which we know by heart. When we return home after an absence, we do not expect to have to remake a place for ourselves. We know "by heart" that there is a place for us.

There are times, however, when this expectation fails, when places we know by heart make a place for us within which we do not feel at home or when they do not have a ready-made place for us, when we are marginalized or even exiled or banished (Said 1990, 357–66). These are the worst of times, because we know, also by heart, that we do not belong. History is replete with examples of how societies have solved the problem of unwelcome difference by marginalizing, exiling, even executing heretics, traitors, murderers, members of other races or religions—and disabled people (Russell 1998).

Adding disability to this list raises the question, How did disability come to be understood as a problem requiring a solution? We organize ourselves collectively and in that organization we generate conceptions about what is valuable and what is not, about what is normal and what is not, and we generate a sense of what is problematic (Smith 1999). Why is disability seen as a problem by itself, isolated from the ways in which societies institutionalize and organize the lives of their members?

Disability is not valued in contemporary society, it is not seen as normal, and it is certainly understood as a problem. No one wants to become disabled and we do whatever we can to prevent it. But if it happens, it happens and we do whatever we can to minimize its negative effects. Disability is not welcome in our homes and we see it as a threat to the structure of our homeland. In the section that follows I take a closer look at the heart of this homeland and how it makes a place for unwelcome visitors such as disability.

Now What?

Using the work of Leo Tolstoy, Max Weber (1947, 143) poses the most essential of all questions: "What shall we do and how shall we live?" Like Hannah Arendt's question ("Who am I?"), this one, too, is asked and answered whenever we act or speak. But since much of what we say and do is done in the "natural attitude" (Schutz 1973) and thus in the realm of what we take for granted, we do not notice this question unless this realm is disrupted. A "now that" is required to make the question more explicit. What do we do and how shall we live now that . . . ?

Disability provides a "now that." What shall I do and how shall I live now that I cannot see line-drives and blackboards? I'm legally blind; now what? I'll eventually lose all my sight; now what? I've lost my sight; now what? Tolstoy's question, posed in the face of blindness, raises the need for decisive action.

At first, I felt uncertainty and fear. Why could I not see the line-drive? What was happening? Was I dying? There was nothing I could do; I was not even sure I was going to live. My parents knew that I was not dying, but they were afraid that there was something seriously wrong with my eyes and they knew what to do—they took me to an eye doctor. The visit to the ophthalmologist removed the possibility of premature death from my mind. I was legally blind and my eyesight would get worse and worse until eventually, sometime in adulthood, I would lose it all. Again, my parents knew what to do. We moved to a big city where I could receive sophisticated and up-to-date ophthalmological and educational services.

The question of what to do was taken care of. My parents, teachers, and ophthalmologists would do the best they could with what they had and so would I. I would do whatever I could with the eyesight I had. At school, I would sit in the front row and I would switch from playing baseball to playing football and basketball. This is what I would do and it seemed to work for a while. My place in the homeland was still secure, a little shaky, but I still had a place. It seemed that I was still

welcome. After all, the homeland was helping me out; I had ophthalmologists, teachers, large-print books. I would get through this; my
homeland was helping.

Around the time of late childhood and early adolescence, however,
things changed and what I was doing became more noticeable to my
peers. They noticed me sitting in the front row and holding books
close to my eyes. They noticed me not playing baseball and not wav-
ing to them from across the schoolyard or street. I noticed the same
things and I also noticed that I could do those things at one time and
could still do them . . . if I could see better.

I was now being noticed as someone who could not do some things.
My private experience of not seeing well was becoming public. I knew
that I saw differently from how I used to see but now I was beginning
to be noticed, and to notice myself, as different from others and this
difference was making a difference. Adults responded to my difference
by helping me, but some of my schoolmates responded by calling me
names. Only much later did I realize that helping and name calling
amounted to the same thing. My schoolmates suggested that I was beyond help; I was ugly and freakish. One boy, combining his beliefs in
the inferiority of women and of blindness, called me "cunt eyes."

This "feminization" of my blindness certainly differentiated me
from my male peers. It was clear to me that I was not just "one of the
guys." I was being marginalized from the "guys." But this marginalization could not be done with eyes alone. Some meaning needs to be attributed to the organic nature of eyes for them to be treated as grounds
for marginalization. The phrase "do not work" applied to eyes means
that people with such eyes cannot do everything that everyone else
does—it means they cannot participate. For young adolescent boys,
participation, in my day, meant playing baseball and sitting at the back
of the classroom. Girls were excluded from such activities. And their
exclusion was organically based; after all, for young adolescent boys,
girls are biologically different and this difference is enough to exclude
them. What better way to exclude a legally blind boy than to feminize
the biology of his eyes? What better way to exclude me from the

"guys" than to castrate me—"cunt eyes."[1] I was being connected to groups of people who, while in the homeland, were relegated to its margins. At the time I did not see the power of such a connection. As a young adolescent boy, I responded, first, with several crying bouts (in the private realm of the feminine), then with several schoolyard and street fights (in the public realm of the masculine), until finally I decided that I needed to change things. Moving to a new neighborhood and attending a new school gave me the opportunity to do so.

Acting as if I could do things and could see in the way everyone else did became my modus vivende. Passing as fully sighted was my answer to Tolstoy's question of what to do and how to live. My experience of being different would remain mine and mine only. My experience of legal blindness would exist only in myself and at home and nowhere else, especially not in my new high school. There, I was like everyone else and not different. Death was no longer a consideration; if anything was dying, or being put to death, it was my legal blindness.

Even though I was not aware of it at the time, my decision to pass was my first political act in relation to my disability. I pushed blindness back to where it belonged, in the private homeland of the self. There was no place for it in the public homeland of sightedness.

I knew this homeland of sightedness by heart. After all, I had lived there for most of my life. I was still living there and, in fact, I had never left. True, my disability changed things but I could still see a little. Before my congenital "eye problem" expressed itself, I was ensconced in the homeland of sightedness in the way everyone else was. I was so at home there that I took it for granted and trusted it with my life; it was my life. Even though my severe visual impairment shook my trust in my homeland, I continued to live there. But now, out of necessity, I would watch sightedness, imitate it, and no longer take it for granted.

As at home as I was in the country of the sighted, I knew that it was not at home with me. If this country discovered that I was not fully sighted, I was convinced, it would banish me in the way it had tried to do when I was younger. Joseph Stubbins, a long-time disability activist, says, "The toughest item on the agenda of disability is that modern America has no need for most disabled persons" (quoted in Norden 1994, ix). Nor does modern Canada. That a society has no need for disabled persons is not surprising. The contemporary obsession with health as well as with the purification and beautification of the body that defines the good life generates a particularly negative view of disability. Not only does a society with such an obsession not need disability, it also feels threatened by it and fears it. It develops all sorts of prevention programs, including those based in genetics,[2] to stave off disability. It places its disabled members outside its conception of the good life, outside its conceptions of productivity combined with those of health, purity, and beauty (Thomson 1997a). Placed in the margins, disability is viewed as bodies and lives gone wrong, as failures of medical science and technology.

This collective marginalization of disability is inexorably tied to the ways in which individual disabled persons conceive of themselves. Collective and individual identities commingle in the living of a life, and this dialectic is the source of whatever version of self we have (Taylor 1989). We rely on collective definitions of Self for our own self-definition as well as for any redefinition of self. This usually implicit process became more explicit to me in early adolescence as I lost my sight and began intentionally to manage my definition of self as a person who was fully sighted. Everyone manages a self (Goffman 1959) and continually defines this self, but this process is usually invisible. Ironically, my blindness made the process of defining a sighted self visible to me. Having approximately 10 percent vision and having been sighted until late childhood were enough for me to define myself as fully sighted and to act as though I were.

At this point in my life, blindness was an individual matter. But I was conditioned by my society to view it as a misfortune. I could not see well; in fact, I could hardly see at all. The things that people around me did, such as read, drive cars, play baseball, and communicate in body language, depended on seeing. Some of these things I could no longer do at all and other things I could not do very well or had to do differently. I could not drive a car and I could not wave to friends across the street as well as other people could. I could read, but only large-print or audio-recorded books. I could make eye contact, but only when I focused my gradually growing "blind spot" on the face of the person with whom I was speaking. But not being able to do some things or not doing them well and doing other things differently from others was not very satisfying. My feeling was that it was unfortunate that I could not see much.

The most salient sense of the world I had during adolescence came to me in terms of a dichotomy: there were those who could see naturally and well and those who could not; there were those who were fortunate and those who were not; there were those who were normal and those who wanted to be; there were my friends, acquaintances, and everyone else and there was me. My issue at that time was not one of self-pity or of hostility or even of bitterness or any other of the psychological responses often attributed to those conceived of as victims of a misfortune. Instead, my issue was living out my life in a world that came to me clearly divided between normal and abnormal. I had an unequivocal experience of my eyesight as abnormal and yet I felt a very strong affinity with the normal world of full sight. I could see hardly anything, but I belonged to the world that could see everything. What should I do and how should I live in this world? Simple, act as if I belong, act as if I can see.

The politics of dichotomy, as Joan Scott (1995, 3–14) points out, is to privilege the first part over the second. My dichotomy of normal/abnormal, which was a derivative of the sighted/blind dichotomy, was not the banal, often perceived as neutral, expression of opposition. Abnormal was not the opposite of normal, for me, nor was blind the opposite of sight. No, opposition had nothing to do with it; sight was the way life was supposed to be, blindness was not. I was supposed to see, I did see. This sight loss was not supposed to happen, not to me.

I knew about blindness long before I began losing my sight. Along with my teammates in Little League baseball, I sometimes called to an umpire, "What, are you blind?" I played blind man's bluff, pin the tail on the donkey, and hide and go seek. Blindness was everywhere; it was a way to call an umpire incompetent or to point out someone's mistake or inability; it was a reason to laugh at someone groping to pin a tail on a donkey or to delight in having the advantage of hiding from the one who was "it." Yes, blindness was everywhere and it came to me in a way that clearly said that the advantage went to sight and that misfortune went to blindness.

In my teens, I saw blind people on television and in the movies and sometimes came across a blind character in a book. They were all portrayed as victims of a misfortune. Blind characters who were able to do or to achieve something that sighted persons do and achieve "normally" were looked upon with amazement by the other characters. Sometimes a blind character would regain his or her sight and always there would be some kind of celebration. People who used wheelchairs or who were deaf (I don't recall seeing a movie or television show in my teens that portrayed someone as Deaf)[3] were portrayed in similar ways.

After moving to the city, I even saw a couple of "real" blind people. I remember being surprised that one of them used a white stick but did not have dark glasses. I thought these two things went together. When I saw blind people in the movies or on television and even when I saw the "real" ones, I saw incompetence, sadness, poverty. And I saw misfortune. Whether my perception was accurate or not is irrelevant; that is what I saw. What I did not see when I saw these blind people is just as significant as what I did see: I did not see me. Still, when I saw them, I experienced a nebulous fear that I later understood was the fear of seeing myself. I was looking at my future and maybe, just maybe, I was looking at my present. I was scared.

As a teenager, however, I could ignore the future and focus on the present. Everyone dies and I too would die, but in the incomprehensible future. Not everyone would go totally blind, but I would . . . in the future . . . and that future was as incomprehensible to me as was my death. For now though, I could see, not much, but I could see. I did not belong where those other blind people did. I belonged here, in the world that sees. As I grew older, however, and lost more sight, another question forced itself upon me: Why me?

Why Me?

This question was more difficult for me to address than Tolstoy's question of what to do and how to live. I knew why I was blind, the ophthalmologists had told me that, but I did not know why it had to happen to me. Knowing *what* was wrong with my eyes did not satisfy my need to know *why* things went wrong.

I did not have a particularly religious upbringing nor was I so oriented in my late teens. Still, from time to time, I wondered whether God had anything to do with this blindness of mine. Did I do something wrong or did my parents? Was there punishment involved? Or, was blindness my destiny? Was I destined to live this life? I did not take these questions seriously and dismissed them almost as soon as I asked them. But they persisted in one form or another. Why me?

I never raised this question with my family. It seemed pointless. Ophthalmologists had already given my parents and me reasons for my blindness. And I never raised the question with my friends. To do so would be dangerous. They did not even know I was blind. Asking them, Why me? would be tantamount to revealing my difference and thus risking marginalization. I kept the question to myself and did so even when, in my early twenties, I gave up passing as fully sighted and began disclosing my legally blind status to new friends and acquaintances. Just as once I had decided to pass as sighted, as a response to Tolstoy's question, this time I decided to get on with life and do the best I could, now that I am blind. My response to Tolstoy's question was pragmatic: I would use my eyesight as much as possible to maintain my residual vision at its current degree of acuity as long as possible; I would read as much as I could using electronic magnification technology and audio-recorded books; I would tell my university professors about my eyesight "problem" so that I could arrange to tape record lectures and invent alternative ways of taking tests; I would be socially active and do things with friends, the same things they (sighted people) did; I would work out physically, running and weight training, and keep my body fit and improve my hand-eye coordination and, oh yes, I would continue to play football. What shall I do and how shall I live . . . now that I am blind? I will do as many things as I can that "normal" (sighted people) do. And I shall live as "normally" as possible. And, I will do this as a legally blind person and not as a fully sighted one. I adopted the macho attitude, no doubt fostered by working out and football, of "a blind guy's gotta do what a blind guy's gotta do." I became an overachiever and focused on the achievements I attained first in sports, and when I stopped playing football, in university. I pushed the Why me? question out of the way. Still, from time to time, it forced its way into my consciousness.

By my late twenties, I was still doing as many "normal things" as I could. I had entered graduate school in sociology and though I was no longer playing football I continued to jog and stay physically fit. The macho attitude I held toward sightedness as an achievement, however, had all but disappeared. I was studying ethnomethodology with Roy Turner and Ken Stoddart and the sociology of knowledge as well as feminist theory with Dorothy Smith. I began "seeing sightedness in a different light" and with a different sense of achievement. Blindness and sightedness soon became primary topics of my research and, using the tools of ethnomethodology, I began delineating how sightedness is achieved in social interaction. With the influence of Dorothy Smith, I also began to think of the social organization and construction of knowledge and the role that sightedness and blindness have in knowledge production.

The work relaxed my determination to achieve the normal things of sightedness and sighted people. People who see recognize themselves as doing so and recognize others as doing so as well. This recognition is not achieved through the scientific tests of ophthalmology; people do not test one another's eyes to determine whether or not they see. Instead, this recognition is tacitly achieved through interaction. Sighted people are unaware of what they do to display the fact of their sightedness to others and to themselves. Who better to *see* this interactional work than someone who is not fully sighted and who has spent most of his life passing as such? Who better to *see* sightedness than someone who was explicitly achieving sightedness in his interaction? I realized that the people who are working extremely hard at "being sighted" are sighted persons themselves. They too are passing! They are not trying to deceive one another, because, after all, they are sighted. But, their sightedness is not self-evident and sighted people must *show* one another that they can see. The self-evident character of sightedness is the product of social interaction. My work also showed me that totally blind people pass as well and that their passing also is not motivated by deception. Instead, they are showing themselves and sighted others that they (blind people) "know" the sighted character of the world and, despite not being able to see it, "know" that the world is seeable. Thus, totally blind people look toward the voice of the person with whom they are speaking in order to make "eye contact." They use language such as "see you later" and engage in many other similar interactions to demonstrate that they know that sightedness is, as Alfred Schutz (1973) would say, "the paramount reality." I began to understand that blindness and sightedness, rather than existing as binary opposites, act together to achieve a sense of reality. I also gained a stronger sense of how the conventional version of the binary opposition of sightedness/blindness privileges the former. This opposition imagines blindness not merely as opposite to sight but as the negation of it, generating a conception of blindness as lack—lack of knowledge, lack of normalcy, lack of ability.

My frantic, macho desire to do the normal things that sighted people do was slowly being replaced by a patience toward sightedness. I was able to watch "sighted work" with patience. Albert Robillard (1999), also an ethnomethodologist, describes a similar orientation. His inability to speak because of paralysis has allowed him to observe the subtle workings of everyday conversation that are taken for granted and not noticed by most. I do not see, Robillard does not speak, and we live in a world populated with people who do see and do speak and who are constantly engaged in concerted interactions that involve doing both. If we are patient enough, Robillard and I can observe the taken-for-granted workings of both speaking and seeing.

> I have come to think of my paralysis as bearing certain gifts. It is certainly not the case that I would not want to be able-bodied again. But I have learned from this experience the power of focused and sustained concentration and

the increased productivity that stems from it. . . . How do I cope with this seeming onslaught? Paralysis has taught me patience. Not being able to speak has been very frustrating. But it has also enabled me to watch the formulation of social structure through conversation, as people talk. (Robillard 1999, 164, 184)

Robillard's sense of disability as "bearing gifts" springs from the paradoxical conceptions of disability, rooted in the Greco-Roman and the Judeo-Christian ethos, in terms that signify the presence of the divine in the profane—either as punishment or as the bestowing of a gift (Stiker 1997). Why me? Because you were chosen; your disability is a gift, a sign of the divine. But this is not the sense of gift that Robillard is talking about. His paralysis is not a "sign from God" or from anywhere else for that matter. Learning is the gift that Robillard is referring to. His paralysis has taught him the power that resides in focus and in concentration and it has taught him that sustaining this power generates productivity. Robillard, to his surprise and probably to the surprise of others, realized that, contrary to the commonsense conception pervasive in our culture that impairment yields inability, which, in turn, yields decreased productivity, his paralysis has made him more productive academically. He is placed in front of his computer at his university office and in that fixed place he and his research assistants spend hours of sustained, focused work. Before his paralysis, Robillard spent much of his time at the university socializing.

I do not have a daily round of chats that I used to have before I became ill. My relative immobility makes it impossible to hop from office to office, meet people in the halls, cross paths with people in going from building to building, attend a number of meetings that I once did, and go to lunches, dinners, and parties. . . . I have developed an amazing ability to return to the spot where I was working before the interruption. I am surprised by this new ability. I did not have it before my illness and could and did get side tracked by discussions with students, usually for the whole afternoon. (Robillard 1999: 92, 93)

Robillard's fixed spatiality paradoxically fixed his focus and concentration. He sits in his wheelchair focused on the underlying and unseen structure of the interaction he once so unfixedly participated in. "Paralysis," he says, "has taught me patience." But he is often very impatient. For example, he loses his patience with those who place him at a social gathering in a position from which he is not able to participate. Robillard relies on hearing conversation and being in visual contact with someone who is able to lip read and translate what he is saying to the gathering. This is how he speaks and when he is placed in a position that cuts him off from such interaction, Robillard loses his patience. His relative immobility may appear to others as though he is patient in the situation, but he is boiling over with impatience.

The patience Robillard's paralysis has taught him is similar to that taught me by my blindness. Robillard must wait for his research assistants to read his lips and to communicate what he is saying to his students in the classroom or to translate what he is saying into papers, articles, and books. I must wait for new books and articles to be audio-recorded or for some one to read them aloud to me before I can read them. These are often tedious processes requiring patience but that often result in frustration. Reading and writing are extremely important to a scholar and, despite the frustrations, they are worth the wait. It may be argued that paralysis forced patience on Robillard in much the same way that blindness gave me a "forced bracketing" (Bakker 1999, 306). My blindness permitted me to "see" sight—it was bracketed from the taken-for-granted work required to make sight appear "natural."

Our patience, however, learned from our respective disabilities, goes deeper than this. It allows us, through sustained concentration, to understand and uncover the processes that go into the social construction of reality. This sensitivity to the subtleties of human interaction, however, is not the sole privilege of disability or the reason for choosing it over nondisability. Despite what he has learned from paralysis, Robillard says, "It is certainly not the case that I would not want to be able-bodied again." To him, "the gift" of seeing the world in a new way is not worth the price of paralysis; moreover, it is possible from the position of able-bodiedness. Having this ability, then, could not be "why" someone is disabled. Not every disabled person sees the world in a new way and disability is often interpreted as signifying that the world is just fine the way it is. This is what medical prevention and curative programs as well as rehabilitation and social assistance programs are all about. Thus every accomplishment of a disabled person is made despite the disability and, therefore, is worthy of praise usually in terms of the strength of the human spirit. On the other side, a disabled person's failure to fit into society or to accomplish anything, according to the standards set by society, is understandable because he or she is not able-bodied. Either way, the dominant ideological construction of the ideal body as "naturally able" is sustained through a conception of disability as an individual "quirk of nature" requiring the hierarchical logic of solution socially organized as prevention-cure-adjustment.

The biomedical model of the human body dismisses the metaphysical question Why me? as superfluous. Hence:

What shall we do now that you are disabled?
We shall cure you.
How shall you live when our cure fails and you are now
    permanently disabled?
You shall adjust.

Biomedicine thinks of the human body as "natural" and, as such, the body is governed by the laws of nature. These laws can be uncovered only by the reasoned (objective) practice of modern science. In relation to humanity, nature is neutral. Why, then, does the human body sometimes go wrong so that some of us acquire blindness or ALS? To the metaphysical question, modern science answers, "No reason." Modernity's view of nature is that it does not operate with human motivations, such as prejudice, revenge, or hate. It works "naturally," without motivation, and sometimes it goes wrong. When scientists ask, "Why?" they are looking for causes. Their inquiry is restricted to uncovering the laws of nature to "explain" how the body "naturally works." Their findings have been translated into the biomedical dichotomy normal/pathological (Canguilhem 1991; Foucault 1979), which allows them to formulate the why question as a question of "cause." Disability, therefore, has nothing to do with the individual. The disabled person is strictly a biological deviation from the "normal body." Even though it does concede that human phenomena such as pollution and poverty may cause disability, biomedicine treats disability as a condition of such human intervention or as an accident of nature.

According to the biomedical model of disability, then, the answer to the question Why me? is contained in the opposition of normalcy and pathology and is expressed as cause and effect. A pathological condition is the cause; my blindness is the effect. The same holds true for Robillard's paralysis. My blindness, his paralysis are abnormal conditions. That is why I am blind and he is paralyzed. There is no other reason.

There is a hegemonic finality that comes with the biomedical model of disability. It advocates the primacy of the "natural body" for the human condition and promotes disability as an unnatural biological condition. This model also suggests that a cogent feature of the "natural body" is its biological flexibility and locates one of the solutions to the problem of disability in this feature. The body will adapt. Hearing will come to the rescue of blindness, sight will save deafness, upper-body strength will improve and compensate for lower-body paralysis, and so on. Disabled people need merely recognize and "accept" the unnatural weakness of their bodies and allow the remaining natural strength of their bodies to compensate. The human body will adapt and it is up to the individual disabled person to "buck up" and rely on the strength of the human spirit so the natural body can do its work.

The biomedical model has been employed pervasively to establish education and rehabilitation programs. These programs are based on the assumption that disability is an individual issue of adaptation and that they are society's way to support such an endeavor. Why me? is never asked within any programmatic expression of the biomedical model. Furthermore, educational and rehabilitative practices never question the value of their existence. Like the natural body, their value is self-evident.

The implication for disability is all too clear; its value is to be found on the other end of the biomedical scale of value. The supremacy of the value of the natural body is at one end of the scale while disability occupies the valueless point at the other. All of the points between these two extremes are invoked by the biomedical model to construct their statistically valuable, yet nonexistent, version of the "normal body" (Davis 1995; Thomson 1997a). There is no flesh-and-bones human body that is normal; the only "normal body" is the one constructed from the "bare bones" of statistics. Biomedicine has authored the fiction of the natural body. "Fiction writer," however, is not part of the self-identity of biomedicine. Its self-identity is, at bottom, that of the "authoritative mouthpiece" of nature. It gives voice to the inarticulate body. Biomedicine renders any other voice inferior to its own (Frank 1991). Its story is *the* story and its word is the final word on the body.

This is the fiction presented to disabled people. It answers every possible question disabled people might have including, Why me? The scientific paradigm contains the possibility for questions, as well as an implicit paradigmatic range of potentially acceptable answers (Kuhn 1962). This paradigm permits the biomedical model to couch the question Why? only in terms of cause and effect. Thus, my blindness is caused by flawed genes. Why me? is also taken care of within the scientific paradigm but in a much more implicit way. The life of the individual is removed in the asking and answering of this question. I have nothing to do with the onset of my blindness since I have no role to play in the configuration of my genetic makeup. My blindness is caused by flawed genes and not by a flawed self or any other kind of self for that matter. Any sense to be made of the question Why me? from the point of view of biomedicine will be made strictly from a historical tracing of the genetic character of my family. Somewhere along the line, through accident or disease, my familial predecessors acquired the genetic predisposition for blindness and, unbeknownst to them, they passed it on to me. No one was responsible.

The entirety of this answer is given silently. I have been examined by several ophthalmologists over the years and have consulted with geneticists. None of these medical practitioners has ever explicitly raised the Why me? question. But the answer was embedded in their talk, which took the form of diagnosis and explanation, constructing my blindness as a feature of my biology and not as a feature of my lived experience. After all, we do not *experience* our genetic makeup unless our experience is received and thus filtered through a biological understanding of what it means to be human.[4] The ophthalmologists and geneticists with whom I spoke, relying on the ubiquitous presence of science in contemporary society and my membership in society, assumed my acceptance of this ideology (Crawford 1980). Their talk was oriented toward giving me a more sophisticated and detailed explanation of my blindness based on the "social fact" that I had already internalized the rudiments of the scientific understanding of the world. Thus, the answer to the question Why me? is that my blindness has nothing to do with me; it is a matter of accident, disease, flawed genes. My blindness is not so much disembodied by the biomedical paradigm as it is "disemselved." There is no reason to search for the origin of my blindness since there is nowhere else to search; the search begins and ends in the body. Other than the mystery in the yet scientifically undiscovered workings of the body, there is nothing mysterious or metaphysical about disability.

And yet, when medical practitioners are done with the body, done with diagnosis, done with their attempts at cure and treatment, they return the body to the self. The self becomes embodied once again but in a body that is flawed. Try as it might, medicine is unable to fix the body and, unfortunate as it is, they must return it to the self, broken.

Here is where the concepts of suffering and victimage fit into the biomedical paradigm. Disabled people are victims of an abnormal body and must suffer this misfortune. Even though the pairing of disability and suffering goes far back in history, predating modern science, the connection is not "natural"; instead, it is generated through paradigmatic conceptions of the world such as are found in biomedicine. The biomedical model is also employed to establish rehabilitation and education programs to "help victims" adjust to their misfortune and to overcome their suffering. The idea is that these programs allow people, drawing on will and desire, to do the best they can with the little they have. Now that biomedicine has done what it can, they relinquish the Why me? question to disabled people with the hope that we will answer it in a way that "will help us" adjust and cope. For biomedicine, then, the metaphysical question Why me? is always-already framed within the pragmatics of Tolstoy's question of what to do and how to live.

This is not to suggest that we (disabled people) always accept the scientific ideology that we are victims and we must suffer. There are times when we become pessimistic, frustrated, and even fatalistic about our disabilities. And there are other times when our disabilities resonate with mystery.

> Being patient and seeing what most people take for granted (and therefore do not see) has not resolved my emotions, however. I am still subject to needs and wants, which I share with most people. I am subject to moods, good and bad. I am in the same social flux as anyone. When I take a reflective step back, usually after a period of stress, I remember that this life cannot be figured out and will always have the moving mystery of the Tao. I can only deal with small features, and then only with those that I have skills for. And even successful dealings will not hide the fact that life is a mystery, like a journey, and that there are no ultimate reasons. (Robillard 1999, 184)

Robillard's paralysis often frustrates him and sometimes overwhelms him. At times, he wonders how he ever copes with it. Despite the patience his paralysis has taught him and despite the insight it has given, his emotions remain unresolved. Robillard's paralysis has presented him with an onslaught of requirements. He must move differently from how he did in his able-bodied days, he must write differently, speak differently, interact differently, sleep, eat, and drink differently; he must live differently. He must do all of this in a world in which most people do these things "normally," in the way he used to.

This world is now Other to Robillard, but not opposite, since he was once this Otherness and still remains part of it. He has needs and wants. He has good moods and bad moods. But, who doesn't? Robillard finds himself in the same social flux that everyone is in. His paralysis has not changed that.

Robillard's paralysis has made him feel different from others and his emotions have made him feel the same as others. All of this difference and sameness, this paralysis and able-bodiedness, cannot be figured out. It is a mystery. Robillard can deal with the immediacy of life, the piecemeal and small features for which he has skills. Stepping back from the smallness of the immediacy of life, however, shows him a mysterious wholeness of life for which he can find no ultimate reason. Why me? Because life is a mystery that cannot be figured out. Mystery, then, is Robillard's story of his paralysis. It is his only answer to Why me?

Arthur Frank (1991) addresses this mystery in his reflections on cancer.[5] Although he believes that it is better to think of cancer as something that "just happens," he admits, "I could not resist asking 'Why me?'" His question, however, placed him on a path that led to the consideration of past inadequacies and guilt and, inevitably, took him into the region of self-blame. Frank does not recommend this path to anyone who has cancer. "As a bodily process, cancer 'just happened' to me. The explanations I like best are fairly medical" (87). Medicine does have its charm. Its explanations of phenomena such as cancer are far more attractive than those to be found in religious ideas involving the omission or commission of acts, which lead to guilt and self-blame. Medicine's neutral physiological depiction of cancer leads us away from such self-blame to the more comforting "just happened." There is nothing we did or did not do that causes cancer; it "just happens" and we are not to blame.

Still, Frank is uncomfortable with this explanation; it suggests a randomness that he cannot quite fathom. "As soon as cancer happened to me, not just to any one, it ceased to be random" (87). Frank conceives of himself not only as bodily processes but also, like all of us, as a consciousness with a will and a history and the ability to focus his thoughts and energies. Bodily process and consciousness do not exist in opposition and, in fact, Frank suggests, "What illness teaches is their unity" (87). He is conscious of his bodily process but the unity of the two suggests more; his consciousness flows through the body and gives the body meaning while being grounded in it. The two interact dialectically, not linearly. "The mind gives meaning to what happens in the body, but the mind also thinks through the body it is a part of. The mind does not simply contemplate itself in a body with cancer. As cancer reshapes that body, the mind changes in response to the disease's effects. Pain taught me the body's power to shape thinking. But my thinking was shaping the pain even as it was being shaped by that pain—the circle is unbroken" (87–88).

The body and the mind (consciousness) are simply not independent of one another as the Cartesian sense of human existence would have it. The two exist together in a way that makes them separable only heuristically. Consciousness is a consciousness both of itself and of bodily processes. The mind shapes the body by giving it meaning and the way it does this shaping is itself shaped through bodily processes such as cancer as well as through the processes we gloss with the idea of "health." For Frank, this is the sort of understanding that can be gleaned (learned) from cancer. Pain puts the mind "in mind" of the body and this mindfulness gives meaning to the pain even as the pain shapes how the mind thinks of it.

There is nothing we can do about the body, it "just happens," but how we experience it is another story. "Illness is a physical process and an experience, each shaping the other. The physical process just happens to me; the experience is my responsibility" (Frank 1991, 88). Ultimately, Frank makes a distinction between the body and how it is experienced. We are born with our bodies; they are a condition of our birth. But even this obvious understanding is so because of the meaning given to the body by consciousness. We are conscious of the body's conditionality and we will make of it what we will from the building blocks of conceptions and collective representations provided us by the society in which we live. Still, we cannot make something of nothing. The body forces us into consciousness and consciousness forces our bodies into meaning.

We ask why: Why this body? Why this disease? Why this disability? Why me? These are not the questions of medical science or of any science for that matter. These are *our* questions as we exist both pre- and postscientifically. These are questions not of scientific discovery but of meaning and as such they are questions of meaning, they are questions that are with us always despite any attempt to bring such questioning to a premature end.

Heart and Home

Why am I blind? and What I shall do? and How I shall live now that I am? are questions that are with me constantly and always. Sometimes I ask them explicitly but most often I ask them in what I say and what I do. Everything I say and everything I do simultaneously ask and answer these questions. When I tediously search for a particular passage on an audio-recorded book, blindness is a frustration; when I say "See you later" to a friend, I merely happen to be blind; when a clerk tells me that the hotel does not rent rooms to blind people, blindness is a societal oppression that I suffer; when I sit quietly behind the backstop of a Little League baseball game, blindness is a lament for a previous and better life; when I think and write about disability, blindness is a teacher and an occasion to think about what is important.

All of these activities, and many more, are conducted in a society and, to this extent, they are collective. Even when I am by myself, I engage in these activities wrapped in the cloak of a collective sense of how the world works and what reality is. I live my life within the natural attitude that freely provides me with conceptions of this reality as well as with understandings of humanity and of what it means to be human. My life is part of the fabric that weaves its way throughout society and provides us with conceptions of what it is to be normal, abnormal, deviant, and it outlines standards for various interpretations of the good life.

Society is replete with conceptions of the body. From the time we are born, we are exposed to a variety of ways to, as Frank might say, experience our physical processes as well as with ways to interpret the processes of others. Our society idealizes the "naturally functioning body" and places tremendous value on the "good working condition" of the five senses. A "healthy natural body" is posited as a prerequisite for a good life and thus as one worth living. It is more valuable and more worthy than the bodily standard to which it is counterposed, the ill, diseased, or disabled body and even the old, overweight, and otherwise not so beautiful body.

This is the society into which I was born and socialized and in which I continue to grow older. This is also the society in which I became blind. My society with its language, norms, values, and beliefs is familiar to me; it is my home. In this home I became blind and continue to be so.

"The vast majority of people who are born with or acquire such conditions [disabilities] do so within families who neither have these conditions nor associate with others who do. They are socialized into the world of the 'normal' with all its values, prejudices, and vocabulary" (Zola 1993, 167). The "world of the normal," that is where I became blind, that is where I am blind. Even though such a world is not an obviously empirical one and thus is one constructed out of particular interests and values, it is the world in which I live. The "world of the normal" is the background against which stands the figure of blindness. This world depicts itself to me as "sighted," now that I am blind. Of course, the world is not sighted, nor is it blind. It does have blind people and sighted people in it, however, and since this "world of the normal" thinks of sightedness as the normal state of affairs and blindness as not, it becomes the "sighted world."

This sighted world is my home, I have no other. But the more I experience blindness, the less "homey" my home seems to be. As familiar as I am with it, I am becoming more and more a stranger in my home. The furniture in my home, once so natural and even so attractive, is now neither. Sometimes I bump into it and other times I stumble over it and there are even times when this furniture brings me to a complete halt. The people of my home often do not notice, and so they do not move the furniture. When they do notice, they most often ask me to go around it and even find ways for me to do so. On those occasions when the people of my home move the furniture, they grumble at the inconvenience and expense of doing so.

Still, this is my home. I belong here, but not naturally anymore. Now that I am blind, belonging is a struggle. First, there is the struggle of pointing out the furniture in the "world of the normal" to those who have constructed it and yet who no longer either see it or realize that they have constructed it. Second, there is the struggle of creating a social identity "out of blindness" as one who is valuable and worth-while. These struggles are political, not individual. They do not, in essence, represent the individual suffering of a condition. Instead, they represent the suffering of a collective whose taken-for-granted di-chotomy of equality and difference is being exposed as artifice by the presence of the difference this dichotomy hides. At times, the "world of the normal" privileges the individual as the source of both social sta-bility and change and, at other times, it privileges society (Titchkosky 1998). This world privileges difference sometimes and equality at other times, but never both at the same time. Difference, as expressed in social categories such as disability, gender, race, is hidden in the world of the normal through constructing the equality/difference di-chotomy and thus reducing the social difference to individual differ-ence. But when individuals "see" their difference as rooted in the so-cial processes of oppression and discrimination, the world of the normal struggles desperately to maintain the view that such difference falls neatly to one or the other side of this preestablished dichotomy. Difference comes down on the side of equality (we are all different but equal as persons) or on the side of difference (we are all unique indi-viduals). This dichotomy hides the essential difference, for example, disability, by formulating the difference of disability as a unique albeit unfortunate condition of the individual. Still, difference persists and much like an individual "fighting cancer" and suffering its pain, soci-ety, my home, continues to fight to keep its dichotomy stable and "normal" and suffers the collective pain that comes from the falling away of a feature that seemed so fundamental, so natural, and so right. I now turn to an interrogation of this sort of suffering in an attempt to depict it as grounded in the social even though suffering convention-ally appears as located strictly in the individual.

3

The Social Location
of Suffering

can remember very clearly the first time the term *suffering* was used to describe me in relation to my blindness; it was during a genetic ophthalmological examination I had in my early twenties. I now think that the clarity of this memory has something to do with the way in which my blindness was presented to me at the end of this examination. I had some indication earlier in my life that my blindness was genetically based, but this was the first time that I had undergone extensive genetic testing. Throughout the procedure, the genetic ophthalmologist referred to my blindness as "the problem" and "the eye condition." So far so good, since this was exactly how I had been conceiving of my blindness. It was something *I had*, a condition, a problem. This "problem" would worsen, I was told, but this was not news to me and so, nothing devastating so far.

But then the "cause," the medical version of "Why?" and "suffering" exploded into the examination results. The genetic ophthalmologist told me that I was "suffering from a genetic eye condition" and that there was a chance, "a two-out-of-four chance," I remember his saying, that if I had children, they would suffer this condition as well. Although the doctor conceded that the choice was ultimately mine, he strongly recommended that I not have children. His words were, "You wouldn't want them suffering what you're suffering."

Things were a little different now, I remember thinking at the time. It was one thing for me to suffer this condition, but for my children to suffer it, that was another thing indeed. My parents had no idea that my eye condition was genetic. They did not impose it on me. It just happened. But now I knew better. Blindness would not *just happen* to my children, I would *give it* to them. Chance was still involved but not in the "just happened" sense. If my children were blind, no one would have to ask why since I would have given it to them. I would be the cause of their blindness. To cause blindness or not to cause blindness, the choice was mine.

In addition to relaying this genetic news and confirming the diagnosis of my blindness, the medical examination reaffirmed what I had known, intuitively, all along, I *had* an eye condition that forced me to do things differently and that I had to get used to and adjust to. Blindness was simply something I had. It was as external to me as bad weather and caused as many problems. The difference was that the weather would get good again, my blindness would only get worse. But now, not only did I have this condition, I could spread it around. My children, their children, who knows how many future generations could also have this condition. As the genetic ophthalmologist said, it was up to me. I could remove the risk and end any future suffering of this condition, at least in my offspring. There was no cure for *my* blindness but I could cure the condition, end it with me. That I have to suffer this condition is no reason for others to.

True, I had suffered my blindness before. I was devastated when I missed that line-drive so many years ago, and I was continually frustrated by the increasing difficulty of catching a football, watching a movie, and doing even the mundane things of everyday life such as crossing streets. There were other problems: I could not read the street signs or the signs on public transportation. Books and all kinds of other print were everywhere. I had to maneuver through this jungle of print and go through the tedious task of finding ways to "read it." I discovered very early on in my blindness that my society was organized by and for people who see and I learned too that no one was about to change this social organization. Somehow, I had to fit in. After all, I was the one with the condition, not society.

These things I suffered; but the genetic ophthalmological examination reaffirmed my blindness as an external condition. This is what I was suffering. I suffered an eye condition that, in turn, caused the condition of suffering I experienced trying to live my life without one of its essential prerequisites, sight. At that point, I was not so much living with blindness as I was living without most of my sight. There was really nothing to think about; I was "without sight" and had to live with that fact. Yet, the ease with which this fact came to me is something to think about. "The apparent ease of intuitive knowledge is really another aspect of discrimination against people with disabilities. How can there be anything complex, intellectually interesting, or politically relevant about a missing limb or a chronic impairment? Pity or empathy do not lend themselves to philosophy, philology, or theoretical considerations in general" (Davis 1997a, 2). I knew intuitively that my blindness was a condition that would bring suffering into my life. After all, my homeland (society) had been telling me this all along. This home I knew so well was populated by "normal" people, who could walk, see, hear, and talk, and scattered here and there among them were a few people who could not. Aphorisms extolled the importance of health and a sound body, and cautionary statements and derisive comments assumed it. "If you don't have your health, you have nothing." "It doesn't matter how much money you have, without your health you have nothing." "What are you, blind?" "Take the cotton out of your ears, what are you deaf?" "She's almost forty; I hope her baby's going to be born okay." "Don't throw pencils, you'll poke out an eye, then you'll be sorry." I heard these expressions everywhere. My homeland was furnished with all sorts of references to the "goodness" of a "normal body" and the "suffering" that was the consequence of an abnormal one. Streetcars were disabled, sports teams had disabled-lists, voices and sound along with print were everywhere and so were curbs and stairs. People "ran" meetings and got "up to speed" and they "stood up" to make a point. They got projects "up and running," they gave each other "dirty looks" and "tongue lashings," they told one another to "smarten up" or to "dumb down." "Be independent," people said. "Where's your crutch, get it yourself!" All of this was everywhere in my homeland. It was apparent and "easy to see" that able-bodiedness was not only the normal life but also the good life and just as apparent and just as easy to see was that disability represented neither. I brought this "intuitive knowledge" with me to the appointment with the genetic ophthalmologist (as well as to every other medical appointment I had), and he knew it as well as I did because he shared my homeland.

As Lennard Davis says, there is nothing complex or intellectually interesting about my eye condition (or any condition of the body), and it certainly had no political relevance. It was straightforward—everyone's eyes worked in the same way and so did everyone's genetic structure. It was simple—find out why my eyes were not working in this way and try to fix them. If they cannot be fixed, I would simply have to suffer the condition, do the best I could with what I had left, and try not to pass this condition on to anyone else. The fewer people with my condition, the better. Evoke the strength of that human spirit and do your best to fit in and, oh yes, keep your hopes up, science might find a cure someday. Simple as that. This was blindness, nothing more and nothing less.

Philology, as Davis suggests, would be of no help and neither would philosophy, unless it was the "positive thinking personhood" ideology disguised as such. Since blindness was simply a condition that "just happened," theorizing was superfluous and would even distract me from the goal of fitting in. I was one of those unfortunate ones and my choices were clear; I could either feel sorry for myself and become one of those blind persons I saw in the movies or I could "buck up" and get on with life. Making the choice was my responsibility, because I was the one who had "suffered this misfortune."

These were the choices available to me during my early twenties. There were no obstacles in my way, only mountains to climb, and reaching the summit, which, by the way, was always out of reach, was worth the suffering of the climb. My blindness was not yet political nor was it anything to think about except in terms of Why me? and What shall I do now that I am blind? It was an individual issue. My home-land (society) remained my home and I needed only to fit in and I wanted desperately to do so. Soon, I discovered that my home was not as desperate to have me as I was to have it.

Why Not?

Not too long after the appointment with the genetic ophthalmologist, which turned out to be pivotal, I began paying closer attention to the ways in which sight was socially achieved. I had, of course, watched sight before, especially during my passing days. Watching sight and remembering what it was like to see were the only ways I could pass myself off as fully sighted. But I was beginning to "look" more closely at exactly how I interactionally achieved myself as sighted and, more important, I began to realize that sighted people also achieve them-selves as sighted and did so in the same way as I did (Michalko 1998). Blindness was not the opposite of sight but was an essential part of it.

What I think spurred me to take a closer look, as much as did any-thing else, was the report by the genetic ophthalmologist and my ex-perience in the days and weeks following the examination, during which I was told that my type of person was not welcome in my home-land. Why not? was the question that haunted me for months after this examination and continues to do so to this day.

Why not? Why not me? Why did the genetic ophthalmologist not want others like me around? More important, why didn't I? Who were we talking about . . . me? Not really; I was sitting in the ophthalmolo-gist's office, in a chair across the desk from him. It was not me we were talking about. The doctor did not suggest euthanasia as a solution to the problem of my flawed genes, nor did he suggest that I "do myself in." Except for their illegality, these acts would certainly have been the most effective solution to the problem of passing my flawed genes on. No, he was not suggesting that. He was not talking about me, the per-son with the flawed genes sitting right across from him.

The genetic ophthalmologist was talking about a type of person. It just happened that I was that type. The doctor abstracted this type from me during our meeting and so did I. I was "a type" and my children, if I chose to have any, could also be "my type." Choosing to have children was choosing to take the risk that they could turn out to be "my type."

What sort of type were the doctor and I talking about? Certainly not a "normal one." We were not talking about blood type or type of hair color—we were not talking about "normal types" that any "normal" parent would pass on to any "normal" offspring. We were talking about a very "abnormal" type, which the doctor and I perceived intuitively as a type that no *typical* person would want to be, including me. At no point during our conversation did I tell the doctor that I did not want to be blind, nor did he ask me whether I wanted to be. Yet, we both knew that I did not. It was, to borrow from Davis, apparent to both of us and "easy to see" that I did not want to be blind. It was just as easy to see that the doctor did not want me to be blind either.

But, blind I was and there was nothing he (medicine) could do about it. What is more, medicine could have done nothing to prevent my blindness. Before my birth, no one had any knowledge, intuitive or otherwise, that my parents' genetic structure harbored a very abnormal gene that would be passed on to me mixed in with all the normal ones. Because no one had such knowledge, my blindness was no one's fault, it "just happened." I had a condition that was generated by the randomness characteristic of human genetics and even though, as Frank (1991, 81) suggests, it was not so random when it happened to me, my blindness was the result of "natural causes" and not of human intervention. The same could not be said of the potential blindness of my children; their blindness would not be so natural. Their blindness would result directly from human intervention and, more precisely, from a particular human's intervention, mine.

Types make an appearance in contemporary society, types that result from accident, diseases that are as yet not preventable or curable by modern medicine, types that come about naturally. As undesirable as these types are and as unwelcome as they are in the homeland of contemporary society, the homeland, for the most part, puts up with these types and lives with them, the best it can. But those undesirable types that are amenable to prevention or cure are another story. The homeland does not have to put up with them. It is not that the homeland views this as a choice; it is not as if there is a choice in preventing or curing an undesirable type (Hubbard 1997). To borrow from Davis once again, the matter is intuitive, the undesirability of certain types is apparent and easy to see. Who would choose to be blind or deaf or paralyzed? What blind person does not want to see or deaf person to hear or paralyzed person to walk? Certainly, no person of whom the homeland of society is aware. Who would want to suffer these conditions if he or she did not have to?

Suffering a condition that can be prevented or cured evokes the idea of choice. Society assumes that everyone places the highest value on the "naturally working body" and that given a choice, everyone would choose this type. Choice, however, is often more implicit than explicit. The presupposition that the naturally working body is the most valuable one as well as the most normal one renders choosing such a body just as natural and just as normal.

I return to this topic in a later discussion but for my present purposes, let me suggest that the issue of choice arises in particular social contexts, such as when we are ill or injured or when we are reminded of our mortality in the face of life-threatening illness, either our own or that of others. These contexts occasion lament and appreciation for the natural body we once had and provide the impetus for healing practices and for the adoption of a life-style aimed at keeping the body as natural as possible. The contemporary trend toward "healthism," Robert Crawford (1980) argues, together with "alternative" health practices, such as holistic medicine and biofeedback, are grounded in the modern scientific conception of the body as natural.

Disability, too, provides a context for bringing the implicit choice of the natural body to the surface. The conception of the body as natural generates the ideology that this body is the only "abled" one. As natural, the body provides us with the "natural abilities" conceived of as absolutely necessary for a "normal life." With "normate culture" (Thomson 1997a, 8) as the ultimate good, the prevention of disability is just as natural as is the natural body. Who would want to be disabled, and what disabled person would not, as Albert Robillard (1999) says, want to be able-bodied again? Choosing a natural body is one thing but choosing a disabled one . . . ? Until my appointment with the genetic ophthalmologist, the idea of "choosing blindness" had never entered my mind. There was no choice, blindness happened to me. Even though there was no cure and I could not return my self to its natural body, I did whatever I could to pursue a normate identity, and I made a point of not "hanging" with any blind people or with any other disabled people. When I did chance to meet someone who was visibly disabled, I felt an inexplicable discomfort. The "world of the normal," to borrow from Zola (1993) once again, was my homeland and because I felt most at home there, I would do whatever I could to "stay at home" as long as possible.

Despite the fact that my home (society) was becoming more and more difficult for me to live in and even though I was beginning to feel like a stranger in my own home, my heart remained there and I persisted in trying to keep heart and home together. A few difficulties and feeling a little strange were not going to force me to move out, and as long as I tried hard and showed that I belonged, my homeland was not asking me to move. In fact, as long as I demonstrated my intuitive knowledge that the "sighted world" was the paramount reality, my home made me feel very welcome, despite my growing feelings of estrangement. I knew that my severe visual impairment was an abnormal condition and so did my home. My home and I both knew that I would not be blind if I had a choice.

This intuitive knowledge that I shared with my home remained unexamined until the appointment with the genetic ophthalmologist. As he gave me the results of the tests he had conducted, he relied on my sharing the same intuitive knowledge about blindness, the body, and society as did he. In fact, the tests, their results, and how the results were presented to me could not have been accomplished without this assumption. The doctor and I relied implicitly on what Schutz (1973, 11–12) calls the "reciprocity of perspectives" regarding normal and abnormal eyesight, which included the privileging of the former and a devaluing of the latter. Ironically, it was this shared perspective that jolted me into beginning to question more explicitly what was "really" being said during our conversation.

Again, we were discussing not me but my type. The genetic ophthalmologist and I tacitly agreed that my blindness was a condition that should be prevented, if possible. The subtext was that my type should be eliminated. This idea of elimination was perplexing and it consumed my thoughts for quite some time. It was the first time I let myself seriously think about my place in a collective within my society commonly referred to as "the blind." I had heard this expression often enough and probably even used it, but it always had an ominous tone and I never associated myself with it. I had no affinity with "the blind" and made it a point not to get to know anyone who did. And, as I thought about the results of that medical appointment, I came face-to-face with the "facticity" (Heidegger 1962) that my affinity rested squarely in the homeland of "the sighted." I realized that I had never before conceived of people as "the sighted" nor did I ever hear anyone refer to himself or herself, or anyone else, as such. There were other groups of people in my neighborhood who were referred to by type— "the Jews," "the Natives"— and, of course, the expression "the wife," which suggests a type rather than a person. But "the sighted" were everywhere and were supposed to be and, therefore, did not notice one another. They were not "the sighted," they just were.

This was the natural state of affairs and my society was trying its best to prevent me from happening again. It could not prevent *me* since I was already there but it could try to prevent others "like me." It was my fate to be relegated to the objectified region of marginalization— into the region of "the blind." The homeland of my society had its borders; there was the center, the "world of the normal," and there was the margin, the "world of the abnormal."

I realized that I had been living in the center by rejecting anything marginal. What is more, my society approved of my doing so. My homeland encouraged me to think of myself as a person, albeit one who suffered a misfortune. But I could overcome it; I was a person with a human spirit and I could, therefore, overcome my unfortunate condition and I would even be looked upon with admiration and I could even be a role model, an example of the strength of the human spirit. The homeland would let me stay as long as I acted upon the intuitive knowledge that this home was the only one worthy of habitation and that all other regions were marginal and largely uninhabitable. As long as I lived as though the "sighted world" was the only world, I could stay.

But the appointment with the genetic ophthalmologist led me to ask Why not? Why not have people like me around? What was it about me and my life that recommended not reproducing it? Why should I be prevented from happening again? The answer is simple: blindness is a condition that deprives people of most, and sometimes all, of their eyesight and, in turn, eliminates most, and sometimes all, of their ability and even pleasure. If people must suffer this condition, then they should do the best they can. But if the condition and thus the suffering can be prevented, it should be. Simple as this answer is, however, it is unsatisfactory, because it relies on a commonsense and, therefore, unexplicated version of suffering.

Suffering

Bill Hughes and Kevin Paterson (1997) suggest that disabled people, especially those involved in the disability movement, abhor the idea of having suffering attached to them. The attachment, it is argued, is offensive because it diminishes and devalues the life of a disabled person by suggesting that such a life must be suffered because of disability, thus implying that disability is a life not worth living and one that must be suffered. No one speaks of nondisabled people as suffering unless a condition interpreted as negative, such as disability, attaches itself to them.

Although suffering is often held to be part of the human condition (if humanity can be spoken of as a condition), it is a suffering that gleans its meaning from the understanding that everyone shares this condition. This general sense of suffering is expressed in particular situations. We all suffer disappointments, losses, the death of a loved one. But, whatever particular form suffering takes, it points to what is viewed as valuable—the value of the thing lost, the value of life, and so on. Thus, the expression "suffering a disability" discursively points to and constructs the value of able-bodiedness while devaluing disability. It implies that disability is a life bereft of value, and not only is this idea offensive to those of us who are disabled but it is also not true.

For these reasons, and I suspect for many more, many disabled people find it offensive to be depicted as suffering their disability. Still, suffering is never absolutely removed from disability, even by the disability movement. Michael Oliver, for example, uses suffering as one of the primary building blocks for the social model of disability. He begins with the definition, conception really, of disability put forth by the Union of Physically Impaired People Against Segregation (UPIAS).

> *Impairment* lacking part of or all of a limb, or having a defective limb, organism or mechanism of the body;
>
> *Disability* the disadvantage or restriction of activity caused by a contemporary social organization which takes no or little account of people who have physical impairments and thus excludes them from the mainstream of social activity. (Quoted in Oliver 1990, 11)

From there he advances a social model of disability in contrast to what he conceives of as its opposite, the "personal tragedy theory" of disability (Oliver 1996, 30). He privileges the social character of disability in opposition to its individualistic character, to what he calls the "individual model" (30). The weakness of the individual model, Oliver suggests, is that it locates the "problem" of disability within the individual conceiving of it as a personal tragedy, "which suggests that disability is some terrible chance event which occurs at random to unfortunate individuals" (32). The social model, while not denying the problem of disability, "locates it squarely within society. It is not individual limitations, of whatever kind, which are the cause of the problem but society's failure to provide appropriate services and adequately ensure the needs of disabled people are fully taken into account in its social organization" (32).

From this, follows Oliver's understanding of disability: "Disability, according to the social model, is all the things that impose restrictions on disabled people; ranging from individual prejudice to institutional

discrimination, from inaccessible public buildings to unusable transport systems, from segregated education to excluding work arrangements, and so on" (33). And, Oliver stresses how his version of the social model of disability is located within the experience of disabled
people in general and within the UPIAS understanding of disability in
particular, which states: "In our view it is society which disables physically impaired people. Disability is something imposed on top of our
impairment by the way we are unnecessarily isolated and excluded
from full participation in society. Disabled people are therefore an oppressed group in society" (quoted in Oliver 1996, 33). Oliver recon-
ceptualizes UPIAS conception of disability as a societal and not an individual issue, as a "social problem" and not an individual one. Colin
Barnes (1998, 78) reiterates the social model of disability.

> The social model of disability is, first and foremost, a focus on the environ-
> mental and social barriers which exclude people with perceived impairments
> from mainstream society. It makes a clear distinction between impairment
> and disability; the former refers to biological characteristics of the body and
> the mind, and the latter to society's failure to address the needs of disabled
> people. This is not a denial of the importance of impairment, appropriate
> medical intervention or, indeed, discussions of these experiences. It is, how-
> ever, a concerted attempt to provide a clear and unambiguous framework
> within which policies can be developed which focus on those aspects of dis-
> abled peoples' lives which can and should be changed.

The social model of disability is clearly a response to the ways in
which society, or in Zola's terms the "world of the normal," conceives
of and treats impairment. The possibility of this conception of society
begins with a sense of an aggregate of individuals who collectively define themselves as existing within a social order (Hobbes 1958; Rousseau 1968). This conventional sociological view of society also posits,
usually implicitly, a collective version of the individual that includes a
sense of the "normal body" (Shilling 1993). Modernity has developed
its own version of society, the individual, and the "normal body" giving rise to the "normate" (Thomson 1997a) as "the good individual"
and to the societal enforcement of normalcy (Davis 1995) upon the human body. Essentially, the body is conceived of in modernity as a biological series of "natural abilities"—the ability to see, hear, walk, and

so on. Finally, modernity "norms" (Davis 1995) the human body and idealizes it (Bordo 1993; Foucault 1980) through "naturalizing" (Frank 1995; Michalko 1998, 1999; Turner 1996) the human body as a societal good.

This construction of the "natural body" reflexively standardizes the body while it is simultaneously employed as a standard to judge the naturalness of bodies. The image of naturalness in relation to the human body generates societal images (or what Baudrillard [1981] refers to as simulacra) of beauty, fitness, health, ugliness, and even disability. The simulacrum of disability paints it with the brush of misfortune, pity, and victimage, yielding a number of contemporary assumptions about disability (Morris 1991, 19–22). Thus, the social model of disability can be read as a response to this simulacrum.

The first item on the agenda of the social model is, as Barnes suggests, to "focus," society's gaze on its role in the social production of disability. Society's focus is on the "natural" or biological aspect of disability and not on its interpretation and subsequent treatment of biology. This focus leads to the "medicalization" (Zola 1977, 41–68) of disability and thus to the medical hegemony of the development of practices such as rehabilitation and education. This focus also constructs disability as a biomedical condition and constructs disabled people as those "unfortunate few" who suffer these conditions.

The social model accepts the "biological fact" of disability but reframes (also a social process) it as "impairment." What it refers to as "disability" are the subsequent exclusionary and discriminatory practices that are a result largely of the contemporary medicalization of the body. Thus, the disabling conditions "suffered" by disabled people are not those imposed on us by our biological conditions but instead are interpretations and images of our impairments imposed on us by our society. It is this distinction that the social model of disability wants to make "clear and unambiguous," as Barnes suggests.

There is nothing we (disabled people) can do about the biological aspect of our disabilities since they are rooted in the "natural workings" of our bodies and minds and are thus unalterable. But, because "what is made" of this biology and how it is socially organized are the result of societal intervention, these "makings" are indeed alterable. Unlike the essential biological "state" of impairment, there is nothing essential about disability conceived of as a socially organized set of societal responses to impairment. Inaccessible environments, pity, charity, and the rest of the array of disabling conditions do not have to exist and, as Barnes says, can and should be changed.

"Suffering," then, is an essential aspect of the social model of disability but it is re-focused. We do not suffer the condition of our impairments as medicine and the rest of society would have it, we "suffer" our society. We suffer what our society makes of our impairments and this, according to the social model, is "oppressive." Any oppression to which we are subject is not to be located in our biological condition but is to be located in the oppressive social conditions created by our society. The emancipatory aspect of the social model of disability is rooted in the understanding that, like any other social creation, oppressive social conditions too can be recreated and thus changed.

Implied in the social model of disability is the social process of "representation." "How we are seen determines in part how we are treated, how we treat others is based on how we see them; such seeing comes from representation" (Dyer 1993, i). Even though Richard Dyer's work involves the visual arts, it is still necessary to "hack a path" through the visual metaphor he uses to represent the "coming to know" and subsequent treatment that exists in the relations between self and other. The social model makes implicit use of such representation in that it "sees" disability as a process of societal representation. The societal treatment of disabled people stems from how it (society) "re-presents" impairment. The process of medicalization, together with the social construction of "normate culture" (Thomson 1997a), once more presents (re-presents) impairment to society, including disabled people, as a "disabling biological condition" that a few "unfortunate people" must suffer and to which they must adjust, the best they can. Representing disability in this way results in "seeing us" as suffering an incurable and thus unalterable biological condition and, in turn, treating us with pity or even with scorn but treating us with admiration if we "adjust well" within nondisabled standards, all with the understanding that, like everyone else, we "hate" being disabled. The ultimate irony is that society "sees and treats" its own re-presentation of disability "as if" it were as natural as impairment. The exclusion of disabled people through the creation of inaccessible environments, then, is "seen" by society as a "natural mistake" at best and as a "natural necessity" at worst.

The social model of disability provides a standpoint from which to glimpse this irony. The sociopolitical conditions under which disabled persons live, conditions often thought of as "natural outcomes" of impairment, are refocused by the social model to present a "clear and unambiguous" understanding of precisely where discrimination and injustice are located. This reframing begins by putting the discipline of medicine in its place. Like medicine, the social model divides disability into its biological and social features. Up until this point, there is no disagreement between the social model and medicine. The disagreement stems from how these approaches differ in their characterization of the social features of disability. Whereas medicine sees the development of prevention and rehabilitation programs as "perfectly natural" responses to impairment and even sees pity and charity as such, the social model sees such responses, especially when they are a result of medicalization, as exclusionary, discriminatory, and unjust.

The essential difference between these two frameworks is that whereas medicine sees responses to impairment (disability) within an ethos of "help" that naturally flows from the natural condition of impairment, the social model sees them as a social creation and thus as responses that could be otherwise. Even though the two frameworks share the understanding that disabled people do suffer, the former sees suffering as the natural result of a biological impairment, and the latter locates it within the social production processes of society. But both the social model and medicine require suffering as an essential feature of their programmatic and practical orientation toward disability. If medicine did not "see" people as suffering their biological impairments, it could not do its work, and if the social model did not "see" disabled people as suffering the socially created conditions of their society, it could not do its work.

Suffering, however, is not the only feature of disability about which medicine and the social model agree. They agree that human biology (the body) is a natural phenomenon. This "natural body" is subject to wear and tear, to aging, and ultimately to death. It is also subject to foul-ups, such as flawed or mutated genetic processes. Accidents put the "natural body" at risk; people sometimes trip and fall, injuring their bodies, for example. The environment subjects the "natural body" to harsh and even hostile climates. Human intervention creates pollution, tainted and unwholesome foods, unhealthy and dangerous working conditions, all of which place the "natural body" at tremendous risk (Beck 1992).

All of these risks, some of which are natural and others not, sometimes result in permanent impairment. Whether impairments result from natural risks or not, they do manifest themselves in the naturally occurring biological mechanisms of the body. My representation of impairment as biology is overly general and extremely simplified. Still, it captures the sense in which both the discipline of medicine and the social model of disability depict impairment by evoking a conception of the body as "natural." Neither approach conceives of the "natural body" or impairment as themselves cultural representations. In Dyer's terms, they both "see" the body as natural and thus "treat" it as such, grounding their conception of impairment as biology. Medicine typically leaves this conception alone, allowing disability to emerge into the social as a strictly biological phenomenon and a subsequent medical problem. The social model, in contrast, conceives of this "leaving alone" not as something passive but rather as an active set of social processes and interpretations that lead to the social creation of disability as only a biological phenomenon and only a medical problem. This difference, however, hinges on the social fact that both approaches see and treat the body as natural and not as social.

The social model's unreflexive acceptance of the body as natural has drawn criticism.[1] Paul Abberley (1987, 8), for example, suggests that the social model needs to "settle accounts with biology" before it can posit oppression in relation to disability. The "naturalization of impairment," a process in which the social model is engaged, presents an impediment to the development of political consciousness among disabled people. "Such a development is systematically blocked through the naturalization of impairment." The social model, Abberley suggests, with its wholehearted acceptance of impairment as biology, prevents any sound formulation of disability as oppression and thus limits development of political consciousness.

Not only does Abberley criticize the social model of disability for not theoretically working out the biological understanding of impairment and thus not "settling accounts with biology" but also he chides the social model for not emphasizing his version of the social creation of disability. Abberley suggests that the capitalist sociopolitical organization of society together with its policy decisions is a major cause of disability. "As far as the majority of the world's disabled people are concerned, impairment is very clearly primarily the consequence of social and political factors, not an unavoidable 'fact of nature'" (11). He refers here to phenomena, such as pollution, unsafe working conditions, and unjust distribution of food, that are consequential of capitalist social organization. Even though he is undoubtedly correct, this version of the social creation of impairment does little to "settle accounts" with biology. It is only impairment, according to Abberley, that is not an "unavoidable fact of nature." But this statement presupposes an "unimpaired biology" that Abberley's formulation tacitly conceives of as an "unavoidable fact of nature." The body, particularly the "natural body," remains for both Abberley and the social model a "fact of nature." The social model treats the concept of the social creation of disability as oppression in that society responds inappropriately to biology, to impairment. In contrast, Abberley suggests that impairment itself is socially created. "Settling accounts with biology," for Abberley, amounts to demonstrating, and doing so quantitatively, that "most" impairments are the result of societal corruption of the "fact of nature," the "natural body." While the social model does "naturalize" the impaired body, Abberley "naturalizes" the unimpaired one. And both evoke the latter—the natural body—as the point of departure for their theoretic and practical work regarding disability.

Susan Bordo (1993, 142) conceives of the body quite differently. To her, the body "far from being some fundamentally stable, acultural constant to which we must *contrast* all culturally relative and institutional forms, is constantly 'in the grip,' as Foucault puts it, of cultural practices." The body is forever "gripped" by culture, and thus, conceptions such as impairment as biology or impairment as a consequence of societal intervention are fundamentally cultural. "Our bodies," Bordo continues, "no less than anything else that is human, are constituted by culture." Culture is always-already "inscribed on our bodies" and therefore, she concludes, "there is no 'natural body.'"

"Natural" is the script of culture writ large on the body. Abberley's work follows this script very carefully; he "directs" it so as to focus our gaze on impairment as the societal corruption of the "natural body." The social model "directs" this script and focuses our gaze on disability as the consequent oppression of society's failure to respond appropriately to the "unnatural body," to impaired biology. Both Abberley and the social model would certainly argue against the conception of the "natural body as normal," but they share in the implicit cultural understanding of the "natural body" of which Bordo says there is no such thing.

Still, we (disabled people) suffer. Abberley suggests that we suffer society's creation of our impairments. In his criticism of the social model as well as of interactionist and other sociological theoretic approaches to disability, Abberley (1998) suggests that rather than liberating suffering, these approaches implicitly sustain dominant societal values. These approaches, he argues (Abberley 1987, 16), "mis-identify" disability as a feature of a few young people, thus ignoring the vast majority of disabled persons who are aged. "One effect of the downgrading of the disabled state is to lead all people, including the 'young' disabled themselves, to deny their own suffering and to normalize their situation, thus maintaining the existing structures of social organization and of work." Abberley is suggesting that theoretic approaches to the study of disability, including approaches within the disability movement, that stress entrée into the labor market and work force for disabled people maintain current dominant values of social organization and work as well as of disability.

Abberley (1998, 92) argues for a more liberative theory regarding disability that develops "the assertion of the rights of the human 'being' against the universalization of the human 'doing.'" He goes on to say that "full integration of impaired people in social production can never constitute the future to which we as a movement aspire." In sum, he says, "We need to develop theoretical perspectives which express the standpoint of disabled people, whose interests are not necessarily served by the standpoints of other social groups, dominant or themselves oppressed, of which disabled people are also members" (93). By understanding the "standpoint" of disability as both abnormal and inferior, the able-bodied standpoint has excluded disabled people from any significant social processes of "being" in the world. "Disabled people have inhabited a culture, political and intellectual world from whose making they have been excluded and in which they have been relevant only as problems" (93).

Whether from the inappropriate responses of society or from exclusion from the "making" of a world that has relegated us to the interpretative category of "problem," we (disabled people) do suffer. Removing the term *suffering* from the referential lexicon for disabled people is an ideological response aimed at combating the ideology of able-bodiedness that conceives of impairment, like illness, as a condition that must be suffered. "Settling accounts with biology," from the point of view of the social model of disability, amounts to accepting a dominant view of impairment as conditionality and biology. However, it re-focuses suffering from impairment to society. The social model does not accept the dominant view, which holds that impairment must be suffered. Instead, it places suffering squarely in the realm of society and its "failed" responses to impairment.

There is a pragmatism to this sort of reasoning. The idea of "suffering an impairment" reduces impairment to an individual matter. Even though impairments can be collapsed into categories such as blindness, paraplegia, multiple sclerosis, people cannot. There is, first, a vast difference in the social locations of experience of impairments among people. The experience of an impairment is influenced greatly by such social factors as age, gender, race, ethnicity, and social class. It varies yet again depending on whether the impairment is congenital or adventitious. Second, the experience of impairment is vastly different even within individual impairment categories. Blindness, as it is defined legally and administratively, for example, ranges from "total blindness" to 10 percent of "normal vision."

Given this incredibly vast range of experience, it would be impossible for people to collect themselves by virtue of their experience of impairment. Even if the nondisabled view were right and people do suffer their impairments, it would be impossible to close the "experiential gap" between a fourteen-year-old with 10 percent of "normal vision" and a forty-five-year-old who is completely blind. The experiential gap of multiple sclerosis that exists between a person from the upper class and one from the working class is just as vast. Gender and race create a similar gap and the examples can go on for a long time.

How, then, can the plethora of experiences be collected? Collecting them is tantamount to treating disability as a social matter and not an individual one. Even though the social model of disability does not address biology and impairments as social constructs, it does provide a way to transform individual experiences of disability into collective experience. It does so by refocusing suffering. Disabled people "collectively suffer" the societal view that people suffer impairments and they collectively suffer the exclusionary societal practices that lead to the development of environments that are inaccessible to disabled people. This version of suffering, which locates disability within the phenomena of "minority group" and "oppression," has, in part, inspired the disability movement.

The social model of disability puts a new twist on Tolstoy's question. Rather than asking What shall I do and how shall I live now that I am impaired? the question becomes, What shall I do and how shall I live now that my society has failed me?

The Path to Social Suffering

Whatever the differences are between the work of Abberley and the work of Oliver and the social model, they all conceive of disability as a form of what Arthur Kleinman and colleagues call "social suffering." Such suffering makes reference to "the devastating injuries that social force can inflict on human experience" (Kleinman, Das, and Lock 1997, ix). Disability is one such human experience translated into devastating injury; it stems from society's construction of impairment as an "abnormal" biological condition in the form of an individual affliction. Society tends to juxtapose impairment to its opposite—"normal biology." A leap is then unreflectively made from "normal biology" to "normal life," leaving impairment behind to "suffer" in the quagmire of an individual affliction and abnormal life. The insidious character of this form of social suffering lies in the fact that it "ruins the collective and the intersubjective connections of experience and gravely damages subjectivity" (x).

Society forces disabled people to conceive of, and subsequently experience, their disabilities as the unfortunate expression of an individual biology "gone wrong" and thus to experience an isolated form of suffering located strictly in the individual. It becomes extremely difficult, if not virtually impossible, to experience suffering as a collective or intersubjective matter. Individuals stay that way—as individuals who possess an impairment and who suffer it in the social isolation created by the "world of the normal" where the nonimpaired biology represents the only legitimate way of being in the world. The American feminist Anne Finger expresses just such a sentiment after the first time she attended a conference of post-polio people.

> I sat for the first time in my life in a room filled with other disabled people. I remember how nervous I felt. Mark was sitting next to me, and I felt glad to have a blond haired, able-bodied lover over at my side. I'd always gone to "regular schools"; I'd been mainstreamed before there was a word for it. I had moved through the world as a normal person with a limp, and no thank you, I didn't need any help, I could manage just fine. And, no, I was nothing like "them." I wasn't whiny, or needy or self-pitying. (Quoted in Morris 1991, 35)

Finger's experience of her disability followed the path that her society carved out. She was a "normal" person, albeit one with a limp. She was not one of "them"; she was mainstreamed, regularized, normalized. Whining and self-pity were not things "normal" people engaged in, especially normal people . . . with a limp.

Until her attendance at that conference, there was nothing collective about Finger's experience of her disability. It was not shaped by a "disability collective"—a roomful of disabled people made her nervous. No, it was another collective that shaped her experience—the nondisabled one. She was intimate with this collective and her blond-haired, able-bodied lover was proof of this. Finger's intimacy with her homeland of able-bodiedness informed and shaped her response to any discussion of the needs of disabled people or of the failure of society to respond appropriately to these needs. She was not one of these whining, self-pitying people.

Confronted with a roomful of disabled people, Finger came face-to-face with a collective, an identity gathered under the auspices of something other than able-bodiedness, disability. Finger was not merely a normal person with a limp, she was a disabled person and this new identification made her nervous. She had followed the path of her society and disability had always been something Other to her.

Roland Barthes (1982, 151), in the language of the 1950s, when his book was first published, speaks of the contemporary social dilemma of the inability to imagine the Other: "The petit-bourgeois is a man unable to imagine the Other. If he comes face to face with him, he blinds himself, ignores and denies him, or else transforms him into himself. In the petit-bourgeois universe, all the experiences of confrontation are reverberating, any otherness is reduced to sameness. . . . This is because the Other is a scandal which threatens his essence." Faced with impairment, contemporary postindustrial society does the same thing; it transforms impairment into sameness. This transformation can be read as an account of Finger's understanding of herself as a normal person with a limp. It also yields the more ubiquitous placement of disability under the umbrella ideology of "personhood," and thus we are persons first and disabled second; we are "persons with disabilities." This formulation finds it impossible to imagine disability as Other to able-bodiedness. To do so would be to threaten the essence of the able body as the essentially "natural and normal body." In the transformation of otherness into sameness, disability is given unessential and conditional status. People have a disability; they are not disability.

This unimaginative relation to disability generates the contemporary understanding of it as "lack" or as "something missing." People with one leg are not "one-legged people," they are two-legged people with one leg missing. People who are blind are sighted people with the sight missing. Their status as people is marked by the signifier of conditionality—person with a disability. They are granted personhood on the condition that they will act as if they were "normal persons with a ————."

Society will do its bit by providing medical, rehabilitative, and special education services as methods for transforming otherness into sameness. Like so many of us, Finger was mainstreamed, regularized, and normalized and her disability was transformed into the condition of a "limp." My blindness was transformed into an "eye condition," one with which my children do not have to live. As a way of completing this transformation, medicine took care of both our conditions. Finger's polio and my genetic eye disease can be prevented. Our "types" can be prevented, but we, ourselves, cannot unless we are "blindly ignored" or we are mainstreamed, regularized, and normalized and thus transformed into sameness.

Still, we suffer our difference; we get nervous in a roomful of disabled people; we fight when we are called names; we wonder why hotels will not accommodate us; we wonder why people stare at us; we wonder why people want to give us cochlear implants; and we wonder why people want to prevent us. And, we suffer these things no matter how "normal" and how "regular" we act.

There are times, however, when we (disabled people) also "blindly ignore" both wondering about and suffering these things. After all, we are sometimes involved in the same unimaginative understandings of our disabilities as is our society. We too at times transform otherness into sameness. We sometimes even say that we do not suffer.

Like Finger's limp, my blindness was Other to me for many years. It was "natural" for me to think of my blindness as a condition and it was quite "normal" for me to experience it as "lack" as well as some "thing" I would rather not have. My heart firmly in the homeland of my society, I ignored my blindness as having nothing essential to do with me and I conducted my everyday affairs so as to transform my otherness (blindness) into sameness and took up citizenship in the homeland of sightedness. I did this first by passing as sighted and thus not allowing my blindness admittance into the social world. Later, when I did "admit" my blindness, I admitted it only as an unnatural physiological condition to which I needed to adjust and with which I needed to cope. I was not going to allow my blindness to threaten my essence or the essence of my homeland. The natural-normalcy of my homeland was secure and so was the natural-normalcy of my personhood. Blindness was merely a condition, nothing that the strength of my personhood and the security of my homeland could not handle. So long as I kept heart and home together, everything would be fine. But I did suffer. It was sheer agony not being able to drive, especially in my teens. I would much rather have been able to watch a movie or play from any other place than in the front row of the theater. Watching my friends playing tennis from the sidelines could not compare with playing. What is more, I was an athlete; I could have beaten them—if only I could see.

I experienced an ever-widening gap between me and my society as my sight began gradually getting away from me. Still, this experience was couched in the ideology of the sighted/blind distinction, with the former conceived of as normal and natural and the latter as not, the former as "good" and the latter as "bad"—blindness was quite simply the lack of sight. The gap between them started becoming an abyss more and more difficult to leap. But my homeland was always "there for me." It would throw me ropes and other paraphernalia to help me make this leap. I even discovered free movies. I got shouts of encouragement from time to time, compassion, and quite a lot of sympathy.

There was no gap between the way I and the way my society understood blindness. Blindness was an unfortunate eye condition. It was also a technical matter and could be overcome with various techniques and technologies. Blindness was a tragedy—a personal one, as Oliver says—that could be overcome by invoking the strength of the human spirit. Any suffering that was to be done was to be done by me. Even though I understood my blindness as a condition that "happened to me" and thus as a tragedy I had to suffer alone, this conception has a collective basis. "Collective modes of experience shape individual perceptions and expressions. Those collective modes are visible patterns of how to undergo troubles, and they are taught and learned, sometimes openly, often indirectly" (Kleinman and Kleinman 1997, 2). The collective I interchangeably call the homeland, society, "sighted world," and "world of the normal" expresses a patterned mode for the experience of disability. Disability is visible to this collective only when it is manifest in an individual or when it is conceived of as a direct threat to an individual; see a person in a wheelchair, see disability; see Down syndrome in an amniocentesis procedure, see the threat of disability. This collective understands the conception of the "natural body" as "normal life" and, from this standpoint, it socially constructs disability as the "personal tragedy" of the "body gone wrong." Not only does this collective patterned mode of experience shape perceptions of how to undergo troubles, it also shapes perceptions of what are considered troubles to be undergone, in the first place.

The existential "fact" of our mortality is not usually experienced as a trouble we must undergo unless we are reminded of it through circumstances such as illness and disability. Disability, however, according to the dominant, nondisabled ideological understanding of the necessity to "undergo the trouble of disability," is a trouble we must undergo; it is the "hardship" that disabled people must undergo in order to "fit into" this "normal world." The conventional sense that disabled people "suffer their disabilities" is grounded in this ideology as well.

But my experience, as well as Finger's, suggests an entirely different sense of "trouble" brought to the fore by disability. This trouble is generated by being with disability. Finger was a normal person with a limp and I the same but with an eye condition. We both went to regular school and we were both mainstreamed not only before there was a word for it, as Finger suggests, but also before we knew we were being mainstreamed. After all, the mainstream was the only stream. Segregated schools or special education classes are not essentially different; they may not have been the "mainstream," but they are certainly tributaries that flow from (and into) it. Both types of education participate in and promote the collective understanding that the only "reality" there is can be found in the "world of the normal" and since this is the only homeland, disabled students should receive all the "help" they can get in preparation for "fitting in."

The standpoint from which Finger and I "viewed" and experienced the world, including disability, was undoubtedly that of able-bodiedness. There was nothing to whine about and nothing to pity; we were "normal" even though one of us limped and the other could not see very much. We moved through the world in our particular ways and with our particular strategies and did so as "normally" as possible.

But then, for Finger, a room filled with disabled people and, for me, a genetic ophthalmologist suggesting that I should not have children, and things changed. We now came face-to-face with disability as a collective construction and we began to understand able-bodiedness as a standpoint. We began to realize that we were swimming in the mainstream. Like real currents the ones in the mainstream of society are often very difficult to detect. They can carry us along without being detected and without too much trouble.

The mainstream is not seen as "main" because it is considered the natural stream of-life that carries all of us along. The mainstream is the only stream and thus the "real" one. As such, the mainstream is not represented as a point of view that generates a particular version of reality—there is no other. Impairment is conceived of as distorting and skewing this mainstream view and, therefore, it needs to be "adjusted" so that it can assume the "correct" point and the subsequent "correct" view. If the adjustment is not total, which it never is, "impaired people" must then be persuaded—through the rhetoric of able-bodied ideology—that their experience of the world is flawed.

Until the appointment with the genetic ophthalmologist, I thought of my blindness as a physiological condition that gave me a distorted view of reality. Since I was the one in possession of this "flawed eyesight," it was relatively easy for me to think of myself as the source of this distortion. Without my particular "looking," seeing would be "normal" and would reveal the "correct" reality. A damaged subjectivity, as Kleinman and his colleagues imply, is certainly a possibility for disabled people. But damaged or flawed subjectivities can be put to one side and disabled people can swim in the mainstream albeit with "bad eyesight" or "with a limp."

It is difficult to say what allows disabled people to recognize the mainstream as an ideology, a standpoint, a social construction. For Finger, it may have been that roomful of disabled people and for me the appointment with the genetic ophthalmologist. My years of passing as a fully sighted person also allowed me to "focus my view" on the mainstream. My training in interpretive sociology, involving a critique of positivistic social science, most likely contributed to the "sharpening" of this focus. But, I suspect that constant attention to the experience of our disabilities and to the ways in which they are responded to by others can bring all sorts of "invisible" things into "view."

Whether it is portrayed in the commonsense and individualistic view of "suffering an impairment" or in the social and collective view of "suffering the failures of society," suffering is an aspect of disability. "Social suffering is a feature of cultural representation both as spectacle and as a presentation of the real. . . . How we 'picture' social suffering becomes that experience, for the observers and even for the sufferers/perpetrators. What we represent and how we represent it prefigure what we will, or will not, do to intervene. What is not pictured is not real. Much of routinized misery is invisible; much that is made visible is not ordinary or routine." (Kleinman, Das, and Lock 1997, xii–xiii). Disability, too, is a feature of cultural representation. The "spectacle" of disability reminds us of the fragile and thus vulnerable character of the "natural body" and its mortality. This representation "prefigures" cultural intervention in the lives of disabled people. Our culture intervenes in disability in the same way it does in anything that is vulnerable and fragile; it tries to fix it (curative and preventative medicine) or make it stronger (rehabilitation and special education) and it tries to help (charity and pity).

This is contemporary society's typical "picture" of disability. This picture is but one frame of the larger picture of the body represented as "natural." This picture is taken from the standpoint of the "natural body" as the only "good body" and the only legitimate way of being-in-the-world. Any picture taken from this vantage point is, reflexively, a self-portrait. No self-portrait of the "natural body" includes disability as a legitimate way of being-in-the-world and since this is not pictured, *it is not real.*

One feature of a culture is that it continuously represents the lives of its people in terms of which type of life is worthy of living and which is not. Disability is rarely represented as a life worth living in our society. For example, the World Bank developed a "metric of suffering" in 1993. Part of this metric includes a scale called "disability adjusted life years" (Kleinman and Kleinman 1997, 12–15). This scale is used by the World Bank to calculate the effect of disability on labor market productivity. The scale is a continuum from "perfect health" (0) to "death" (1). (Interestingly, the World Bank places blindness at 0.6 on this scale.) As extreme as this representation of disability is, however, it is no less extreme than depictions found in other cultural representations, such as the print media, film, television, and other promulgators of popular culture (Gartner and Joe 1987; Klobas 1988; Mitchell and Snyder 1997). Even more highly regarded arenas of culture, such as higher education, generate negative representations of disability (Titchkosky 2000).

All negative cultural representations of disability simultaneously picture the "natural body" as "normal life" and thus as the only life worth living. It is no wonder that many disabled people find life in the mainstream so compelling. The normalizing and mainstreaming of disabilities, such as a "limp" or "bad eyesight," are methods ubiquitously available to disabled people for positioning themselves into the "view finder" of the camera (cultural representation) that takes the "picture of normal life." Unlike the other (natural body), whose position in this picture is taken for granted and not even noticed, the disabled body must actively position itself into the "frame" by demonstrating its commitment to fitting into the "world of the normal." It is this social sense of belonging to normalcy that is so compelling to many of us. "The notion that someone with a very visible physical disability might "come out" perhaps seems oxymoronic to those for whom the cultural assumptions that structure the normal remain unquestioned. Indeed, pressures to deny, ignore, normalize, and remain silent about one's own disability are both compelling and seductive in a social order intolerant of deviations from the bodily standards enforced by a quotidian matrix of economic, social, and political forces" (Thomson 1996, xvii).

It would seem that someone who is "very" visibly disabled is already "out." In fact, to and of such people, "normals" often say, "I don't even think of you as disabled," or, "You know, I sometimes don't even notice her disability." And visibly disabled people themselves, tacitly acknowledging their disability, often say things like, "I'm a person, just like you. Treat me as a person."

As visible as some disability is, it is very often denied. Denying and ignoring one's own disability in the face of the collective Zola calls the "world of the normal" is nothing other than the process of normalization, of fitting in, and many disabled people do it extremely well. But fitting in is possible only when the "voice of disability" is silenced. Indeed, silencing the voice of disability is a, if not the, key cultural assumption that structures the normal. Silencing the voice of disability and keeping its standpoint invisible are fundamentally necessary for denying and ignoring the social fact that normalcy is socially structured and produced with an implicit set of assumptions. Silencing the voice of disability allows normalcy to speak and to do so as though with "one voice." All voices are heard as one and otherness is denied and ignored and transformed, as Barthes says, into sameness.

Coming out, in Thomson's terms, goes far beyond the notion in popular psychology of admitting one's disability or the rehabilitation notion of accepting one's disability. Indeed, these two notions themselves silence the voice of disability by privileging the reality of normalcy and the subsequent need for disabled people to fit in. This version of accepting one's disability amounts to the privileging and acceptance of normalcy as the only "reality."

Coming out is a political matter and not a psychological one since it is a social process that "outs" normalcy. The ideals of the "natural body" and of "normal life" are indeed compelling and even seductive, as Thomson says. Still, they are ideals in as much as they are "normed" within the social construct of the "natural." Conceived as "natural," normalcy can hardly be anything other than compelling and seductive.

Part of the seductive character of this "ideology of the natural" is its compelling argument that the human body is adaptable and flexible. When disability enters this picture, it is represented as a "misfortune" to which the body can adapt. Disabled people need only accept their abnormal conditions as "individual tragedies." Disability then becomes a "personal problem," as Oliver says, and in the context of postindustrial society disabled people can make use of techniques and technologies that will give them an entrée, albeit a marginal one, into the mainstream. The mainstream with its ideology of the "natural body" remains so and disability presents no challenge since it is seduced by this ideology and compelled to conceive of it as naturally normal.

Coming out as disabled, however, means to "come out" of this picture of "naturalness" and to question the conditional character of impairment. This questioning is achieved through suspending the tacitly held assumption that identity is connected to disability through the condition of impairment. The conceiving of impairment as a biological condition generates disability as a condition as well. Disabled people are then thought of as "people with ———"; people with limps; people with eye conditions; people with multiple sclerosis; people with a condition. This implies that disability is not itself an identity since it is only a condition that affects identity conceived of individualistically as a "person."

Coming out as disabled implies the necessity of reconnecting disability and identity. It is to ask Nancy Mairs's question, "Who would I be without multiple sclerosis?" (1996, 9). It is to ask Oliver's implicit question, "What's the connection between my society and my disability?" It is to ask Finger's question, "Why am I so nervous in a roomful of disabled people?" And, it is to ask my question, "What does my society have against my type?" The question is not, Do disabled people suffer? instead it is, What do disabled people suffer? This chapter represents my attempt to ask this question and to provide some basis to begin to address it. "Outing" the conception of the "natural body" as an ideology and a social construction brings disability back as a voice and an interlocutor in the conversation of the meaning of humanity. It suggests that the meaning of disability is steeped in the process of social relations (Karatheodoris 1982) and that how we conceive of disability will shape how we represent and treat it, whether our own disabilities or those of others. In the next chapter I show how disability is a social identity and that what we, disabled people, suffer forms such an identity and gives it shape.

4

Coming Face-to-Face with Suffering

As obnoxious as the sensation is to me, I did suffer my blindness and still do. At the beginning, I couldn't play baseball anymore; I simply couldn't see the ball well enough. I didn't like this and I disliked even more "watching" my friends play. I remember my uncle soothing me and saying that I would make a great little second baseman. I didn't like this much either, but I didn't tell him. I knew I could play second base; I did, I still could. I could play, but I also knew I couldn't and I knew why and it wasn't because I couldn't play second base. I didn't like this either. Many years later, this feeling came back when I was watching my friends play tennis. I knew I could play and I even knew I could beat them. Yet, I knew I couldn't.

I remember not liking school much either, especially in junior high. Everyone, particularly boys in those days, sat in the back of the classroom. It was cool to sit back there. I had to sit in the front and I even had to walk up to the blackboard to see it. This was not cool. I had the same feeling; I could sit back there, but I couldn't.

Driving though, or more correctly not driving, was the hardest thing of all. Same thing, I could and I couldn't. Everyone else could drive and everyone, again especially boys, wanted to. At around age sixteen, driving a car was a huge deal in my neighborhood and high school, and it sometimes seemed that that was all we ("guys") talked about—who had his driver's license, who had a learner's permit, who had access to a car, what sort of car, what sort of car we would like to have, and on it went.

Social scientists are probably right that driving a car represents some sort of rite of passage from adolescence to adulthood. It certainly did in my neighborhood. Since I was totally immersed in passing as fully sighted at that time, not driving was extremely problematic. Driving itself was the problem, however; many of my friends and acquaintances did not have a driver's license and even some who did had no access to a car. The problem was having a "good reason" for not driving. Even though being legally blind was reason enough, using it as such was definitely not part of my strategy for passing as fully sighted.

Thankfully, however, the culture that put so much pressure on me to pass as "normal," also presented me with the structure and organization from which I could create a "good reason" for not driving. I lived in a lower working-class area of the city where quasi-delinquent behavior was quite acceptable and even appropriate. It was not difficult for me to create a "good story" for not driving from the building blocks of this social context. Caught drunk driving by the police and having the right to hold a learner's permit suspended for a year was a story that worked well enough. Another story could be fabricated from the same building blocks in another year.

While this story was interactionally sufficient for my continuing "to be" fully sighted, it did not do much for me personally. I really wanted to drive, to be normal, to see. There was no rite of or any other kind of passage for me. I passed from sighted to legally blind quite easily; it "just happened." Later, I passed as sighted by interactionally accomplishing sightedness and even though this was not quite as easy as becoming legally blind, I did do it. But driving a car was another story. I could drive; my father showed me how in the empty parking lots of early Sunday mornings. Still, I could not drive. I passed from sightedness to legal blindness and, from there, I passed to interactional sightedness. But I could find no passage that would get me to driving. I did not have the right to take this rite of passage. I imagined my uncle soothing me and saying that I would make a great driver some day but I knew I could not drive and I could not play second base.

The "problem" of my blindness during adolescence was knowing that I could do things and thus knowing that I was as "good" as anyone else . . . but not quite. I had a strong feeling of disingenuousness back then, brought on by the constant vigilance required to pass as fully sighted together with its subsequent anxiety. But it seemed just as clear to me that my homeland expected me to be "normal" and this expectation meant nothing other to me than "being sighted." My homeland expected to be populated by "normal people" and I saw no signs that it expected "abnormal ones" to show up (Michalko and Titchkosky 2001). Furthermore, when they did show up, my homeland was not ready for them. There were no accommodations for those in a wheelchair or those who could not see or could not hear. Clearly, my homeland did not expect "these people" to show up and when they did, my homeland did not change much. It seemed as though "these people" had to either "get through" or "get out" and sometimes the two amounted to the same thing.

Adult Suffering

But what of suffering now that I am an adult? It is quite easy to understand the trauma that is experienced by someone who loses his or her sight in childhood. It is just as easy to understand how a teenager is compelled by the desire to be like everyone else or, as Colin Barnes (1996, 37) says, "to be one of the lads." It could be argued that the seduction of sameness is strongest during adolescence. There is a sense of "liminality" during this time, as some anthropologists argue (Murphy et al. 1988; Turner 1985). Adolescents stand waiting on a threshold, seduced by adulthood and compelled to cross over. But does this sense of liminality cease when the leap into adulthood is made? Are there other thresholds to cross in adulthood? Is the view of adulthood from the threshold of adolescence all that there is to see? Does this adolescence/adulthood dichotomy have any consequences for disability?

It would be relatively easy, as well as tempting, to respond to these questions directly by simply answering them. Liminality, it could be argued, does not cease in adulthood insofar as there are many other thresholds to cross, such as the development of personal relationships, child bearing and rearing, and career choices. And, it could be said, the view of adulthood that adolescents have is adolescent in that their understanding of being an adult is romantic or scary or otherwise incomplete (Michalko 1984, 296–311). And surely there is a difference between an adolescent experience of disability and an adult one; we might say the intensity of the peer pressure to conform during adolescence is proof enough of this difference.

But these straightforward answers blur the meaning that resides in the adolescence/adulthood dichotomy. The conventional understanding of this dichotomy, while located in the "problem of difference," presupposes and thus ignores its meaning by invoking the life cycle as the solution to this problem of difference. Thus, adolescence and adulthood become two distinct, yet inseparable, stages of life. Adolescence is seen as a temporary stage on the way to adulthood, yet connected to it, since the experiences of adolescence are brought into adulthood. Conceiving of life as a passage through stages generates both the adolescence/adulthood dichotomy and the meaning we attribute to each. Growing up/grown up, immature/mature, irresponsible/responsible are but a few of the obvious distinctions we make between these two stages of life. There is a sense of "incompleteness" surrounding adolescence and one of "completeness" for adulthood.

This version of adolescence and adulthood lays the ground for the teenage experience as one of turmoil and anxiety, especially when it is seen to correspond to the disruption of the body caused by major biological changes during adolescence. The girl is becoming a woman, the boy a man, one identity is being replaced by another; this is the meaning presupposed in the adolescence/adulthood dichotomy. It is the meaning inherent in the problem of "identity-difference." The passage from one identity to another is always disturbing. One identity is being left behind and the one now taken up often seeks to disrupt the former and sometimes even to destroy it; hence the admonition often given to young adults: "You're an adult now, act like it." Or the one sometimes given to those in late adolescence: "As long as you're living under my roof . . ." Both these admonitions, which, notice, come in the form of reminders, rely on the problem of identity-difference for their possibility.

This problem (assuming a new identity) gives rise to the anthropological notion of rites of passage. People pass from one identity to another and if a culture deems an identity to be significant, rituals will be developed to accompany this passage. Descriptions and analyses of such rituals abound in the anthropological literature (Turner 1985). We need only turn to our own cultures, however, and our own lives to see them. Prime ministers and presidents are installed, people have wedding and anniversary parties, students graduate, people get new jobs, people celebrate birthdays and attend wakes and funerals . . . and, oh yes, people get driver's licenses.

We encounter many "identity crossings" in our lives and some of them, if they are important enough, are ritualized. We expect that we will take some of these crossings, such as crossing over into adulthood, and we wait on the threshold preparing for our first step into a new identity. But there are other identities for which we do not wait and into whose province we do not expect to traverse. Some make us shudder when we think of them as a possibility and we dismiss such thoughts from our minds as quickly as possible. Disability is one such identity.

Disability is a unique identity category. For one thing, it is "open-ended" (Gadacz 1994). Everyone, as Irving Zola (1982) says, is only temporarily nondisabled. Anyone may become disabled at any time. Such a possibility, however, evokes anxiety and fear in much the same way as does the inevitability of death. Thus, cultural rituals, such as wedding ceremonies, are employed to clarify the blurriness of socially acceptable identity crossings but not for the crossing into the identity of disability. This crossing takes time, because it is a social process and not an instant leap from one identity to another. In the same way, crossing from "straight" life to "gay" life, also a social process, often takes years and the precise moment for such a crossing is not usually identifiable.

Because contemporary society is reluctant to endow disability with the social category "identity," crossing into it is not merely a journey bereft of a clear path, it is a journey sometimes not even embarked upon. Many of us, of course, can clearly identify a point at which we acquired an impairment. Some of us are told that we were "born this way"; others know the time and place of the accident that "caused" their impairment; still others know when they had a stroke; and some of us even remember not seeing a line-drive. But there are many more who are convinced, usually by others, that they are "stupid" until they discover that they have a "learning disability." Many are convinced, again usually by others, that they are "hysterical" or "hypochondriac" until they discover that they have multiple sclerosis.

Still, knowing when an impairment occurred or being diagnosed with one does not itself represent a crossing of identities from nondisability to disability. There is no such crossing, because there are no such identities. Disability is not typically conceived of as an identity but neither is able-bodiedness. Both are conceived of as "states" and "natural ones" at that. The biological conception of the human body treats it as nature and thus as "naturally given." It treats the impaired body the same way, even though it is tainted with "nature gone wrong" and thus "unnatural." There are no social identities to be found anywhere in what is naturally, or unnaturally, given. Biology and medicine typically represent the body as tabula rasa and whatever text is found on it has been written by the human artifice of culture and society. There is no writing and no artifice to be found anywhere on this "natural body." Biology and medicine place disability more in the realm of nature than in the realm of social achievement. Social identity is a matter for human artifice and not for nature; even genetic predisposition must be expressed in human society.

The concept of crossing between nondisability and disability according to this perspective is framed within the "natural movements" of the body. People "move" from having eyes that work to having those that do not, from legs that work to those that do not, from ears that work to those that do not. Some are even born with body parts that do not work. The "trick" is to "make them work" but, failing this, people are destined to "suffer" their naturally nonworking bodies and to adjust to them as best they can.

Within this conception of the "natural movement," there is no particular identity for those with impairments or even for disabled people. The social model of disability does allow disabled people to identify with one another by virtue of the oppression we suffer at the hands of a society that has created a human artifice (environment) that excludes impairment. This environment dis-ables us and, much in the same way that the "disabled" streetcar stands frozen between the need to move and the inability to do so in the streets of Toronto, we too "stand" frozen in the gap between the need to participate in society and the inability to do so. If the disabled streetcar is to move, it is to move in the same way that nondisabled ones do. The same sort of logic is applied to disabled people; if we are to move in our society, we are to do so in the same way that other members do. We may need some "assistive technology," a few curb cuts and even a few accessible public transportation vehicles, and as long as these accommodations are "reasonable" and not too expensive, and as long as they do not transmogrify the environment, we will move, perhaps not quite in the same way as others, but we will move. In this movement, however, there is no identity and there certainly is no "standpoint of disability" to which Paul Abberly (1987) alludes (see Chapter 3). There are no disabled people in this picture, just "differently abled" ones. We move through the environment in the same way as other members do because, "essentially," we are the same as they are, we are "persons," and, albeit differently from them, we are also "abled."

I walk down the street in the same way that everyone else does except I am with my guide dog, Smokie. I teach sociology at my university in the same classrooms as do my nondisabled counterparts and we even teach the same students, most of whom are nondisabled. Of course, unlike the other professors, I tell the students that raising their hands to ask a question is futile. I use a dictaphone designed exclusively for people who see to write and to make notes. I sometimes use a computer, also designed for people who see except, every now and then, mine speaks. Even though I do them "differently," I do the same things that nondisabled others do. So, what is the difference? Nothing, really; I am just a person who is "differently abled."

Correct as this depiction is, it somehow does not ring true for me. In the midst of this sweepingly smooth and milky-sweet fog of sameness lurks the figure of difference. It sometimes springs from this fog so forcefully that it cannot be denied. My difference sometimes seems very stark to me. New articles, new books, and new work are all around me. Other professors go to the library, go to the bookstore, secure these new works and read them. I check; are these new works available on audio tape? If so, I wait to receive them. If not, I wait longer. Other professors collect term papers, take them to their office, and grade them. I need to make a complicated set of arrangements before I am "able" to grade term papers . . . "differently." Other professors convinced university departments of their qualifications for "getting the job." I did this, too, but I also had to convince some people that blindness does not prevent me, or anyone else, from teaching at a university. Some believe this, most do not. "My professor is a hard marker," a student says. "Mine is blind," says another.

This figure of difference is with me always in my sameness. But it comes to me in still another way; one that is much more ambiguous and very elusive. It is not the figure of difference that springs clearly into my life in the form of the "need" for assistive technology and mobility guides and the necessity for arranging "things differently." "Meeting these needs" allows me to do my work and allows me a path, albeit one strewn with obstacles, to cross the threshold into "ordinary membership" of society. This clearly defined figure of difference also provides me with the impetus to persuade my society to remove some of the obstacles from this path.

I no longer have the adolescent need to pass as fully sighted. I have made the move to adulthood. Still, things are not all that different. I am no longer passing but I am still open to the seduction of the "normal world" Rosemarie Garland Thomson (1997b) describes and I am still compelled by its lure of ordinary life. This is, in some ways, not very different from the adolescent desire to be like everyone else. The deep, visceral need to belong, as Cornel West (1995, 16) puts it, is still strong despite the move to adulthood. Yet, this figure of difference does represent a kind of "coming out." I am blind, everyone knows, and I do not keep my blindness from anyone.

But, I am still not sure of what exactly has "come out." In adolescence, I passed as sighted so that I could be the same. Now, in adulthood, I do things "differently" to the same end. The difference is that, in adulthood, I have allowed my difference to "come out" in the form of a technical problem. Doing things technologically differently from others is now represented as the key solution to the problem of blindness. This version of the "problem" can also be extended to society as a whole by suggesting that the technical removal of obstacles and changes of attitudes toward disabled people is the solution to the problem of disability. And there is nothing incorrect about this formulation either.

If this solution were to come to fruition, it would effectively silence the voice of difference in disability. There would be integration and full participation of disabled people in society. We (disabled people) would no longer identify with one another on the basis of oppression. This account would have been settled with society. Liminality would no longer be an existential condition for disabled people. We would no longer be on the threshold of participation in society, we would be participants. This solution suggests that the difference between disabled and nondisabled people lies in the opportunity to participate in society. If society organizes itself so as to provide this opportunity for both, the difference is removed.

Still, I do not see what others do: Thomson appears (very visibly) physically disabled and Finger still "walks with a limp." Participation notwithstanding, what difference do these differences make? Are we different? Do we identify with our differences? Necessary as it is to "settle accounts" with society, it is also necessary to "settle accounts" with difference.

Identity and Suffering

One of the most "abnormal" things about being "normal" is attending to its production. Once this is done, normalcy loses its self-proclaimed status of unreflexive naturalness. Normalcy blends into what is conceived of as "naturally given" and the only way to sustain this camouflage is for it to avoid any attention, especially its own. The humanities and social sciences have a long and well-known history of attending to the normal. The animating question for sociology since the time of Saint-Simon and Comte, for example, has been, How is society possible? Philosophers of the modern age asked a similar question. René Descartes wondered what counts as indubitable knowledge. Nietzsche, and later postmodern philosophers, raised the question of perspective in human life. Until recently, however, this attention has restricted itself to human action and has excluded the body,[1] as in Max Weber's famous distinction between "behavior and action." This ilk of attention to normalcy as human action assumes a taken-for-grantedness of the body as a relatively stable set of unstable physiological processes. Thus, the study of the body was left to the "natural sciences" while the humanities and social sciences focused on human action in relation to nature.

Through the conception of "social construction" the latter focus included the constant of the natural body by suggesting that its meaning flows from human interpretation. Beautiful and ugly bodies, ill and well bodies are matters connected to the social construction of nature. The body thus is understood as a constant set of building blocks upon which such interpretations are constructed. As I show in the previous chapter, however, even the natural body is sometimes seen as an exclusively human phenomenon in that it, too, is the "script of culture."

That we interpret our bodies and those of others is undoubtedly true. As the social model of disability so poignantly points out, impaired bodies are given negative interpretations by contemporary society. But, like much of the humanities and social sciences, this model also suggests that impairment (the body) resides in the domain of nature and that the negative interpretations of such bodies (disability) are the domain of the social. A "disability consciousness," then, is located in the social and not in the natural region of impairment. Whether there is "no natural body," as Susan Bordo says, or whether there is one, as the social model of disability says, the consequence for disabled people is the same: we must focus, or refocus, as Colin Barnes says, our gaze on what culture and society make of our impairments.

Making something of the body is an activity conducted in the confusing space between nature and culture. The confusing space between the normal and the abnormal is similarly the "work place" in which "societal stuff" is made of our impairments. It is within this space that concepts of disability are developed by society. Now developed, however, disability remains in this confusing space and disabled people are forced to live a life in this space, between nature and culture, normal and abnormal. Is it I who is abnormal or is it my impairment, my body that is? Or, is (n)either abnormal? Certainly something abnormal is going on since I am raising such questions. What sort of a consciousness is this? I rarely hear sighted people raising such questions. To borrow from Martin Milligan's "brilliantly clear vision," sighted people simply "live in their eyes" (Magee and Milligan 1995, 45). Their life is in their eyes; they see themselves in one another's eyes (Cooley 1909). Their identities are in their eyes; their world comes into their eyes; they "live in their eyes." They construct a world, natural and otherwise, taken for granted, "in their eyes." The confusing space between nature and culture is "cleared up" and fused in the distinction between the two that exists "in their eyes."

But the confusing space between the abnormal and the normal remains for disabled people.

> The disabled person always fuses the physically typical with the physically atypical. The disabled body is also often merged with prosthetics such as wheelchairs, hearing aids, or white canes. Disability is also sometimes experienced as a transformation, or a violation, of self, creating classification dilemmas, ambiguous status, or questioning assumptions about wholeness. All persons with physical disabilities thus embody the "illegitimate fusion" of the cultural categories "normal," which qualifies people for human status, and "abnormal," which disqualifies them. Within this liminal space the disabled person must constitute something akin to identity. (Thomson 1997a, 114)

The elusive "figure of difference" to which I allude in a previous discussion resides in this liminal space. Out of the complex fusion of typicality and atypicality, as well as of normalcy and abnormalcy combined with the transformed and often violated self, the disabled person must carve an identity. Moreover, this identity is constituted within the nature/culture and the subsequent impairment/disability split, which suggests that the experience of impairment (the body) is existentially different from that of disability (society). Thus, who I am is what is made of my impairment.

But if, as Milligan says, sighted people "live in their eyes," where do blind people live? Common sense along with science tells us that blindness is the negation or lack of sight. Much of what we experience and know, they argue, comes from the sense of sight. These two perspectives make a distinction between the world and the sense-perception of it, and thus they would never answer the question of where blind persons live since they would never pose it in that way. Disagreeing with Milligan, common sense and science would say that sighted persons "live through, and not in, their eyes." Their question would be, "Through what do blind persons live?" And predictably, their answer would be, "Through hearing, through touching, through their remaining senses." This reasoning presupposes a clear distinction between the world and the body connected by the thread of the subject/object dichotomy—the world is a common object perceivable and knowable by a subject through the "common senses."

But these distinctions are not as clearly given as common sense and science would have it. The distinction between the world and the perceiving subject as well as the one between the body and the self are not so separable and are actually quite blurry. Arthur Frank (1998, 209) says, "Culture inscribes the body, the body projects itself into social space, and the boundary of these reciprocal movements is in flux." Culture inscribes my blindness in the script of disability but my blindness (my body) projects itself into the social space of such inscribing activity. The boundaries of this space are in flux.

"Bodies are in," says Frank (1990, 131) and by particularized extension I would say, "so are eyes." Like bodies, eyes are in, "in academia as well as in popular culture" (131). The academy has developed an interest in the "place of the eyes" in contemporary society (Foster 1988; Jay1993; Jenks 1995; Mirzoeff 1998) and popular postmodern culture, with its character of the simulacrum, privileges the "image as visual" (Baudrillard 1990).[2] It is not difficult to "see" that our contemporary society "lives in its eyes" as well.

I too live in my eyes, albeit differently at different times, and these differences are what blur any distinction between my impairment and my disability and also are what keeps the boundaries between them in flux. Like anyone else who is sighted, I lived the first ten or eleven years of my life in my eyes. But then I experienced a dramatic "loss of sight." I could still see, but not much. I lived in "partial sight" and, for many years, relied on this partiality as well as on memory to "live in the eyes" of my world. "Life in my eyes" certainly characterized my years of passing as fully sighted. I live now with almost no sight (light perception) and I move in the world with my guide dog, Smokie.

Living "in eyes that do not work" does not mean that I do not live in my eyes, for I still do. My identity resides in my eyes, despite, or perhaps because of, their nonworking status. I live disjointedly as an instrumental actor trying to "see" a world with these eyes. The world comes to me as "dysappearance."[3] "Life in my eyes," ensconced in the blurry memory of appearances, transmogrifies these appearances into the dysappearances of "what I see."

My eyes, in contact with Smokie's eyes, guide me across the border into the "world of appearances." We are cautious; we are vigilant; we walk with a precision known only to us. We walk, blind man and dog, culture and nature, through a world from which we are ordinarily estranged and yet through a world with which we are extraordinarily familiar (Michalko 1999). Smokie and the life in my eyes have both been "domesticated" in and by this world of appearances. This is our domicile, our homeland, and yet our life in it resonates with the trepidation felt by those who move through a land to which they no longer and not yet belong (Arendt 1955, 4).

I move through the world with my eyes, with the memories of eyes from another time, and with Smokie. Much of my movement is instrumental; after all, the "eyes of my homeland" are watching. Will I make a mistake? Will I get disoriented, or worse still, lost? Will I bump into one of the homeland's many appearances? The homeland is concerned and watches to make sure that I have "figured out" its intricate arrangement of appearances. Most important, the homeland watches to make sure that I do not mistake my dysappearances for its "real appearances." I too am familiar with these appearances and I am also watchful of any mistakes I might make. Everything becomes a "cue" for appearances and everything, including appearances themselves, signify appearances. Whatever appears to me in the "world of the normal" does so as a signifier of "what is really there." I see a wisp of cloud pass by me on the sidewalk; but not really, since I immediately begin to "look" for what it signifies: Is it a person, a post, a no-parking sign? Is it a telephone booth? These are the things that belong on a sidewalk, not clouds, and when I see a cloud, I look for these other things.

Sounds, smells, my "distant sense" (Howes 1991) of touch from my six points of contact with my world (my two feet and Smokie's four paws)—all of this floods through me as I move through the world. This experience comes to me not so much as a smooth flow of sensibility but as a kaleidoscope of sensation, a kaleidoscope made up of all of the senses, not just sight.

With Smokie and with the memories of the eyes of another time, I have sorted out many of these kaleidoscopic dysappearances. Many of my wisps of clouds have taken on the shape of other significations. The thin, tall, and darker clouds are posts of one type or another . . . usually. The ones that are not so tall that move with a more erratic wisp are people . . . usually. A darting movement to the side from Smokie and then back again tells me we have just moved around something— perhaps a sandwich board advertisement or a person standing still or an open car door or perhaps just a piece of paper or a twig Smokie thought I might trip on. A sudden and sometimes barely perceptible flow of air and we have reached the end of the buildings on a sidewalk and in a few feet Smokie will stop at the curb of an intersecting street. The wisps of clouds are now cloud formations and the kaleidoscope of dysappearances take on an order, an apparent one.

Still, my kaleidoscope retains some of its kaleidoscopic character. Some of the clouds remain cloudy and mysterious. "What was that?" I ask Smokie as we pass one of them. "What could that be?" I wonder as another "cloud of mystery" makes an appearance on my horizon while we stand waiting at an intersection for the traffic light to turn in our favor. "Who was that?" I ask Smokie, as we pass by a "Hi" emanating from a group of wispy clouds. Smokie sometimes unravels the mystery of clouds, especially the clouds he likes. He sometimes moves gradually, almost hesitating, to the edge of the sidewalk and stops in front of a low and dark cloud. I reach and touch the stretch of shrubbery he has found there. Laughing, I remove his harness and, while I hold only his leash, Smokie sniffs, pees, and takes a respite from his work of moving me among and through the clouds.[4]

Sounds, smells, and the ever-present "feel" of Smokie in his harness as he extends my sense of touch—all of this is my world. But it is not the world of my homeland—that I need to "figure out" from my world conceived of by me as a kaleidoscope of cues and signs. My world is the signifier, my homeland the signified.

There is a temptation, one to which I often succumb, to conceive of my environment instrumentally and to treat it almost exclusively in that way. It is tempting for me to "see my seeing" as a world of dysappearances that, although themselves not real, point to the real ones and thus to the "real world." This temptation does have its drawbacks, because in the process of "figuring out" what is "really there," I am in the constant presence of potential mistakes, some of which represent potential danger to both Smokie and me. But there is the other side; it is fun to figure things out and my environment often comes to me as the most complicated of all puzzles with Smokie, my memories, and stock of commonsense knowledge and my "kaleidoscopic seeing" as clues. Either way, I am instrumentally involved in piecing the puzzle of my environment together.

The most salient feature of this puzzle and of my figuring it out is blindness. I move through the world "blind-ly." I am with and in blindness as I move (Michalko 1998, 1999). I insert blindness into the world as yet one more piece of the complicated puzzle. But Smokie and I (as blind) never enter a world bereft of blindness. Blindness is always-already in the world in the form of cultural representation. This cultural representation is also in me. As Frank suggests, culture is inscribed on my body—my blindness—and I project this "body of blindness" into social space. My culture, together with Smokie and me, reflexively inscribes blindness on and into social space.

This activity, too, has its drawbacks; some cultural representations of blindness make moving through the world quite arduous. There is the ever-present ethos of "help" and the equally ubiquitous sentiment of "pity" that greets Smokie and me as we enter the world. People often grab my arm and offer me help in crossing a street, more often than not a street I do not wish to cross; a few people have offered me money; others offer prayers; still others speak of the good fortune of their "gift of sight"; and some, of how they have been graced by God, saying, "There but for the grace of God go I," and they say these things in a stage whisper as Smokie and I pass by; a few even express their amazement at Smokie's prowess at guiding. All of this encompasses the social identity "ready-made" (Taylor 1989) for me as Smokie and I enter social space. This is the identity I suffer daily.

But there is also a humorous side to "walking into" such an identity. After all, identities can be ironically mirrored and reflected back to the world. There are times when I meet a person for the first time or speak with a stranger on the street that my blindness becomes a topic. Some will ask me about my "eye condition" and once in a while, but often enough to make me "blink" with wonder, some ask whether I have "seen an eye doctor." Irony comes in very handy in these situations. I tell them "No, I've never thought of it!" Inevitably, they laugh, apologize, and chide themselves for asking such a question.

But what remains? What is left unspoken and unseen in this story of figuring out the "real world" and of suffering a pregiven marginal identity? What is this story about? Is it a parable? a fable? Does it bear a message, itself to be figured out? Is living in the clouds merely living in the literal difference between sight and blindness? Is this difference only physical? Or does it bear a metaphysical mark? What of the freedom from signposts, from curbs, and from the body itself, which is "seen" only when one is in the clouds? Can freedom from the hegemonic hold of the natural body be secured by anything other than disability? Disability is not merely a reminder of the fragility and mortality of the body; it is the standpoint from which we are free to view the body as the multitude, diversity, and possibility of movement; it is the view that sees the restricted and limited version of movement that springs from the impairment of "body natural." Physical movement is cloaked in the mystery of clouds. Let me now demonstrate what happens when such mystery is removed, when disability is ignored.

Facing Suffering

The beginning is a good place to start and this story begins with the hard fact of eyesight and the equally hard fact of the physical and social environment. It turns out, though, that the "fact of eyesight" is not all that firm. It happens, so the story goes, that some of us actually lose it. Eyesight is very fragile and is vulnerable to disease, flawed genes, and accident. It is a gift, and if we are not careful, we can lose this "gift of sight" (Levin 1988, 56). This story begins, then, with the loss of this gift.

And what of the hard fact of the environment? It is very hard, harder than eyesight, and even harder than it appeared at "first glance." No fragility here, and the environment, especially the social one, does not seem to be vulnerable to anything, or so the story goes. Enter blindness. And with it the return to the hard fact of eyes, but this time to the incurable hardness of eyes that do not work . . . naturally. So there we have it, the two protagonists of this story; on one side, the hard and immutable social world and on the other, the hard and immutable fact of blindness. And, oh, how they suffer each other.

This suffering takes the form of the superior/inferior relation. The facticity of the physical and social environment is taken for granted and is understood as "just there" for anyone to "see." The "just thereness" of the environment is achieved through what Hans-Georg Gadamer (1975, 19–28) calls "*sensus comunus*," a combination of the common senses of the body and the common stock of knowledge of culture.

Thus, the environment is not only understood as a hard fact; it is also "seen" as a "true thing." As a true thing, the environment is itself true." It does not lie; it presents itself truly to those with naturally (true) working senses and with a common (true) stock of cultural knowledge.

Blindness, however, presents a threat and a challenge to the superiority of this true thing, the environment. While the environment is just there for anyone to see, it is only truly "just there" for those who "can see." It can make an appearance only when appearances can be "commonly sensed." Blindness generates only dysappearances and, from the point of view of sight, blindness cannot "see" the "truth" of appearances. Blindness is a reminder to sight of the fragile vulnerability of eyes and, since blindness is typically conceived of as happenstance, it also reminds sighted people of the risk of going blind. Blindness is a threat to both seeing and appreciating the world decked out in its true-thingness splendor.

But the threat runs a bit deeper than this; what if blind people actually believed what they saw? What if we thought we were actually seeing the true thing? Then there would be two true things—one "seen" by common senses and another "seen" by uncommon senses. The world would appear in one way to sighted people and in another way to blind people and, as radically different as these two worlds would be (are?), they would both be true things. But our society, steeped in Aristotelian logic and the philosophy of the Enlightenment, will have no such thing: "You cannot have A and not A at the same time," and "You cannot have a sighted world and a nonsighted one at the same time either." Modernity conceives of the idea of multiple realities in terms of opposition as well as in terms of contradiction; reality is One and only one true thing. There is no blending or synthesis of multiple realities for modernity, since reality is a monologue and not a dialogue.

The challenge that blindness presents to the commonsensically organized social world is to convince its members, including its blind ones, that the essence of blindness is nothing other than biology "gone wrong." This demonstrates that, far from being *sensus comunus*, blindness is "really" *sensus privates*, a pseudo reality generated by the private experience of blindness. The concept invoked as a way to signify this state of "biology gone wrong" is impairment, which is understood, even by the social model of disability, as an individual and not a collective "problem." This understanding is rooted in the biological gloss "human biology" that defines the "human condition" as the shared condition of nature expressed in the naturally occurring biology of any human.[5]

Any individual or group differences in this shared condition can also be accounted for biologically. A shared biological condition conceived of as "normal" is not understood as having a "cause" since it is understood within the paradigm of "nature," and, from an empirical point of view, a phenomenon cannot cause itself. The cause of nature thus cannot be located in nature. But differences in biology have a quite different biological frame. Human difference such as that found in height, hair color, and eye color are seen as quite "normal" and as part of the "normal variation" of human beings. But other differences are not so "normal." They are biologically framed within the "abnormal"—as disease and mutation. Unlike "normal biology" and its "normal variation," these differences are conceived of as caused. Nonimpaired biology "happens" and, depending on one's perspective, it happens usually either naturally or supernaturally. Either way, modern science cannot attribute cause to either of these two perspectives because they too would have to be caused and this would lead to the unfathomable sense of infinite regress. Thus, even though modern science is animated by the understanding that the workings of nature can be understood, the causes of such workings cannot be definitely established. "Normal human biology," "normal biological variation," and even "nature" itself, then, are interpretive, metaphoric representations of the Realness of human life and for the understanding that while the "workings" of this Realness can eventually be understood, its cause and "nature" cannot.

This depiction of the paradigm of human biology is undoubtedly overly simple. My purpose, however, is to deconstruct the "natural body" and thus to provide grounds for understanding the "impaired body." This deconstruction suggests that while impairment can also be framed within the concept of "biological difference," it is certainly not an aspect of "normal biological variation" as is eye color, for example. Variation in eye color does not represent an impairment as long as the color falls within the spectrum of what biology understands as "normal biological difference." Typically, however, eye color does not make a "social difference." Of course, when eye color is combined with skin color and when these traits are combined with some genetic or supernatural sense of who counts as human and who does not, a social difference is made—racism. But in terms of the five senses and the natural way of seeing the world, eye color makes no difference. In contrast, a significant variation in the number of rods in the retina or the presence of pigmentation on the macula, for example, does make a difference. The difference is that, unlike eye color, these conditions often cause blindness.

A different set of appearances appears to people with these "eye conditions" than to those without them. This difference amounts to living in the same world as does everyone else but "seeing" it differently. I am not using the term *seeing* metaphorically here; I am not suggesting some ocular centric notion that generates contradictions in knowing and believing. I am not speaking of hegemonic visual metaphors, such as, "I see your point, but I disagree." Or, "From my point of view, I see a completely different reality than you do." Instead, I am speaking about the differences in the sort of "vision" that different eye physiologies permit. That I "see" clouds where others "see" people or sign posts is not a reflection of differences in our standpoints or even of our social location. When I "see" clouds, I "know" and "believe" that I am "looking" at something else. I am looking at what everyone else is looking at, but I am not seeing what everyone else is seeing.

The question now becomes, What difference does this difference make? What difference does it make to me when I see clouds where others see sign posts and what difference does it make to them and what difference does it make to us? The common sense of sight along with commonsense knowledge permits people to see sign posts while the uncommon sense of blindness, together with the same commonsense knowledge, permits the same sight. In this, there is no difference between blind and sighted people. When I see a cloud, I know I am looking at a sign post, or at "some such thing," and herein lies the difference. When I see, I know I am looking at "some such thing" yet to be determined, figured out, whereas when sighted people see, they know they are looking at "some particular thing" always-already determined and without the requirement of "figuring out."

Still, we are looking at the same thing and the difference is that we are "seeing it" differently. But, this difference is more radical; while we see things differently, I am wrong and "they" are right. The difference our difference makes is that *I am different*. Even though "we" claim to see differently from one another, only my difference counts as such.

The difference I experience in the context of blindness and sightedness is not that of the one between points of view. We can rationalize our points of view and argue for their superiority over others. We hold opinions and beliefs that may differ from those of others. Despite these differences, and despite arguments we may have with others regarding these differences, we continue to hold opinions, points of view, and beliefs and we may even change them from time to time.

The difference my blindness presents to me and to the rest of the world, however, is a different matter. When I say I see clouds on the street, for example, I am not starting a discussion or inviting an exchange of opinions. I do not expect to hear in response, "No Rod, I think that's dust being blown up by the wind." My seeing clouds is nether spoken nor heard as opinion, belief, or point of view. The speech genre (Bakhtin 1986) of discussion or exchange of opinions does not mark the social occasion of my difference. But, what does mark it?

Useless-Difference

The difference of blindness is located in the understanding that blindness resides in the genre of difference that does not make a difference. It is not the insertion of a new (different) point of view, belief, or opinion into the world. The world remains the same, it is no different now that blindness is in it. Blindness merely conjoins with the already existing genre of the possibility of distortion. The world is "just there" for anyone to "see" and this "seeing" is predicated upon a perceptual apparatus that does not produce a "distorted look." The biomedical version of blindness—the "look" that blindness has of (on) the world is not new and different; it is the "distorted look" or, more poignantly, the "look of distortion."

There are no clouds on the street, standing still, moving, or speaking. There is no almost imperceptible breeze between the end of a row of buildings on a street and an intersection. These are only distortions, for there are only sign posts and people on the street and only buildings and intersections. My blindness and thus "my look" does not make a difference; there are no clouds on the streets for others, now that I am looking. Neither a different aesthetic nor a different utility are inserted into the world when I look since what I "see" comes from the "look of distortion." Despite the radical differentness of my "look," no difference is made; the world remains the same. Blindness is thrown on the heap of "useless-difference."

In the "face-to-face" (Levinas 1969) of blindness and the world, there is no essential difference, since blindness is distortion. The modern world is open to, and welcomes, new discoveries and new perspectives, but it is not open to and does not welcome differences that distort.[6] This is what grounds the suffering that blindness engenders and, perhaps, what grounds the suffering of all disabilities. We (disabled people) suffer our difference in the face of the Other as a difference that does not make a difference; we suffer our useless-difference.

Suffering, says Emmanuel Levinas (1988, 156), "is at once what disturbs order and this disturbance itself." Disability is much the same. It certainly does disturb order represented as the physical and social environment, including those for whom this environment is intended. This "order" is the imaginary of, in Irving Zola's terms, the "world of the normal," where what is imagined is an edifice conceived of as the "normal world" constructed by and for "normal people." Since it cannot, this world does not imagine disability as an integral part of itself, and when disability shows up, not only is it unexpected but also it disturbs the "world of the normal" at all levels of its consciousness.

Disability is certainly disturbing at the level of individual consciousness, both for those who are disabled and for those who are not. It is disturbing to be marginalized in a world in which your heart is firmly entrenched, in a world you experience as your homeland. It is more disturbing still to realize that your sensorium or your body "sees" differently or "looks" different from what is expected, including from what you expect.

Nondisabled people are disturbed by disability. It reminds them of the fragility and vulnerability of their existence and reminds them of their mortality as well. Furthermore, nondisabled people are often very uncomfortable in the presence of those of us who are disabled. They patronize, pity, and even ignore us. Many times Smokie has guided me to the door of a public building where I have "groped" for the handle of a door being held open for me by a silent someone doing a "good deed." Of course, this good deed effectively achieves and perpetuates the disturbing character of "the groping blind." It is disturbing to watch a blind man approaching a door and it is disturbing to "know" that he will "grope" for the handle and it is disturbing (somehow) to tell him that you have opened the door for him. To open the door or not to open the door; both are disturbing, for the man is blind. Asking him whether he would like you to open the door may be disturbing to the blind man, but a closed door may be disturbing to him as well since he will have to grope for the handle. Ignore the blind man: let him, or better still, someone else, deal with the door. Still, you are right here, you should hold it open. What to do? This is all very disturbing.

At a more collective level of consciousness, things were going along quite well, at one time. Sure people had accidents or contracted diseases, and sure, some people were disabled by these things and there were some who were even born disabled. But there were "special places" where *they* could live, "special schools" that *they* could attend, "special places" where *they* could work and all kinds of "special stuff" that *they* could do. Now, this was not disturbing to anyone, well, maybe to *them*, but *they* were already disturbed. It was not as though *they* were not being taken care of; *they* were with *their* own kind and, moreover, with our help *they* are living the best kind of life *their* limitations allow. This is the best situation for all concerned.

But then, someone, somewhere had the bright idea" that *they* should live in the "world of the normal." Some even said that *they* had a "right" to do so.[7] And things got really disturbing. The disturbance was in the disability itself. Disability reminds people of something they already know about but would rather act as though they do not—their mortality. What is disturbing about disability, then, is that it disrupts this "acting as if" by reminding people of the fragility of their existence. Furthermore, people know that the membership category "disability" is always open and is open to anyone. The presence of disability reminds people of this fact and this, too, is disturbing.

Since disability is so tightly bound to the biomedical model of the body in contemporary society, it is almost impossible to conceive of it as a category of societal membership. Like Emmanuel Levinas's conception of suffering, disability is understood and experienced as nothing other than a disturbance to the "normal" biology of the body. It is conceived of not as a collective matter but as an individual one. This reasoning holds that disability is collected under the category of "population," not of "people"(Foucault 1980, 25). There is a "disabled population" and not a "disabled people." (I say more about this in the following chapters.)

Thus, disability conventionally represents a disturbance to individuals and to a population. Individuals take precautions against becoming disabled and populations take precautions against having a "high rate" of disability. To both groups disability is a disturbance to be avoided and, as such, it is usually not thought of as a category of societal membership with "human rights." Instead, disability is often conceived of as a strictly biological matter that results in negative consequences for an individual, requiring the consequential act of "humane treatment" rather than "human rights." This is why the fight for disability rights has taken so long and why legislated disability rights is so often not enforced.

What the nondisabled other suffers in the face of disability, then, is the suffering that comes from being present to one experienced as a "victim of misfortune." The difference of disability thus becomes the useless-difference borne by anyone victimized (disturbed) by misfortune. Individual strength and the degree of humane treatment exercised by a society toward misfortune become the only measures of how well either individuals or a society lives with disability. This provides at least a partial response to Zola's question regarding why society excludes so many of its members.

> Suffering, in its hurt and its in-spite-of consciousness, is passivity. . . . Is not the evil of suffering—extreme passivity, impotence, abandonment and solitude—also the unassumable and thus the possibility of a half opening, and, more precisely, the possibility that wherever a moan, a cry, a groan or a sigh happen there is the original call for aid, for curative help, for help from the other ego whose alterity, whose exteriority promises salvation? It is the original opening toward what is helpful, where the primordial, irreducible, and ethical, anthropological category of the medical comes to impose itself—across a demand for analgesia, more pressing, more urgent in the groan than a demand for consolation or a postponement of death. (Levinas 1988, 157, 158)

Thus,

> The inter-human lies also in the recourse that people have to one another for help, before the marvellous alterity of the Other has been banalized or dimmed in a simple exchange of courtesies which become established as an 'inter-personal commerce' of customs. (Levinas 1988, 165)

The "extreme passivity" by which Emmanuel Levinas characterizes useless suffering may also be located in the difference of disability. What difference, for example, does someone's blindness make—to that someone or to how that blindness is "seen" by others in the world? Is blindness "seen" as a "unique look"? Or, what difference does wheelchair use make? How is someone in a wheelchair "seen"?

If blindness and wheelchair use are "seen" strictly and only as deviations from "normal seeing" and "normal mobility," then the ground for useless-difference and thus passivity is laid. Those who are blind and those who use wheelchairs are "restricted" to the difference-of-deviance and need only fit into, or be fit into, the identity and life ready-made for them in and by the world of the normal (Titchkosky 2000). The passivity of this "fitting into" is found in the fact that a place has been ready-made for disability in this world. The difference-of-disability makes no difference to the world of the normal and the quintessential place of this world remains, despite disability, the hegemonic ideology of "normalcy." The "view" from blindness or from a wheelchair makes no difference since it has no value as a view. The "sighted world" sees blindness as distortion and the "walking world" sees wheelchair use as confinement. Both are seen as misfortune. Blindness is understood as "impotence" with respect to "normal seeing" and the same holds true for wheelchair use with respect to "normal walking." Both are seen as the misfortune of solitude conceived of as confinement—the one bound to "not seeing" (*sensus privatus*), the other "wheelchair bound" (*corpus privatus*).

The ideology of nondisability as normalcy symbolically constructs disability as, to continue with Levinas, "abandonment." Some "natural" ability or function has abandoned someone; eyesight has abandoned the now-blind person and the "natural" ability to walk has abandoned the person now "bound" to a wheelchair. The former is "confined" by a "distorted look" and the other is confined by useless legs. What remains is a life conceived of as the "task," often thought of as a laborious one, of living with confinement. The difference-of-disability is thus understood as a useless-difference—living with useless eyes, with useless legs.

But then there is Levinas's sense of the Other, of alterity, of exteriority; there is the sense of the other to disability that is clearly nondisability—useful eyes, useful legs. This Other is not confined to those others concretely seen as nondisabled people. While it includes these types, the Other is given birth and informed by the ideology of nondisability, of the "natural body." It is the inscription, to return to Foucault, of culture writ large on all of our bodies. But this inscription is easily erased. Disability itself, as Lennard Davis (1995) suggests, is a reminder of the fallibility of culture's inscription; it is erased as easily as it is written. But the script cannot be erased. The cultural script of the "natural body" remains indelibly with us regardless of and in spite of the particular condition of our bodies. The "natural" (nondisabled) body is with us, one and all, disabled and nondisabled. Naturalness is not to be found in any particular body; it is the exterior, alter (body), the Other found written on every particular body.

The moans, cries, groans, and sighs of suffering to which Levinas refers are heard emanating from those whose inscription of naturalness (of humanness) has been erased. In the face of this erasure stands the exteriority and alterity of the other holding out the "promised salvation" of "aid and curative help." Face-to-face, disability and nondisability "stand" opposed, the latter suffering the useless-difference of the former. The difference-of-disability makes no difference to the "natural Other" except to remind it of the fragility of life and the need to end the "useless-suffering of useless-difference" with aid and curative help. Thus, disability is an "unworthy difference" that generates both the meaninglessness of useless-suffering and the ethical requirement to remedy it. The contemporary biomedical response to disability is not only grounded in this version of the difference-of-disability, it also perpetuates this difference and produces the disability/suffering connection as a "natural" one.

The biomedical ethics of remedy ("curative help") represents a "bad will" toward the recognition of any meaningful difference that disability might make. "This bad will," Levinas (1988, 158–59) writes, "is perhaps only the price which must sometimes be paid by the elevated thought of a civilization called to nourish persons and to lighten their suffering." Levinas conceives of this bad will as the "uncertainty" of modernity in the face of suffering. The opening of an ethics of the "inter-human," according to Levinas, originates in the "suffering of suffering" where one "justifiably suffers" the useless, and thus unjustifiable, suffering of the other. Thus, "the very phenomenon of suffering in its uselessness is, in principle the pain of the Other" (163).

The pain (suffering) of disability can now be seen as socially located in the Other. It is nondisabled others who suffer the difference-of-disability. Disability, understood as useless-difference and unjustifiable suffering is what generates both the biomedical ethics of remedy and the commonsense response of pity. Understanding the idea of suffering a disability, therefore, requires us to interrogate the scene in which disability appears. This scenography (Butler 1993) does not seek to dismiss or destroy the notion of "suffering a disability"; instead, as I try to show, it aims to deconstruct this notion, thereby laying out the scene that provides for the possibility of any connection between suffering and disability.

This deconstruction brings to the fore a more social sense of "suffering a disability." Some disabilities include the suffering of physical pain but all disabilities include an orientation to, and in many instances, a suffering of "the suffering of suffering." This means that disability is understood in contemporary society as an "unjustifiable condition" of which some people are "victims." Disabled people thus suffer the social category and orientation of victim. This suffering expresses itself most often in the response of pity experienced by disabled people in the face-to-face interaction with nondisabled others. It generates clichés, such as, "I've still got all of my senses; knock on wood," or "Be thankful for what you have because that can happen to anyone." Disability as memento mori springs from this version of "suffering a disability," and thus disability becomes a reminder both of the fragility of the human body and of how fortunate or graced are those who are not disabled.

This version of "suffering a disability" not only "hears" disability as a "cry for help" but also yields a particular orientation to what counts as "help." Recall Levinas (1988, 165): "The inter-human lies also in the recourse that people have to one another for help, before the marvellous alterity of the Other has been banalized or dimmed in a simple exchange of courtesies which become established as an 'inter-personal commerce' of customs." Understood as victimage, disability becomes, as Michael Oliver (1996) says, an individual or personal matter. It becomes a matter of finding a cure, of adjusting, and of coping, a matter of all the techniques and technologies so "customary" to the disciplines of medicine and rehabilitation. It becomes a matter, too, of the form and content of interaction between disabled and nondisabled people. "Common courtesy" is one such interactional form. "Don't stare, it's not nice." "Just be lucky *you* can walk." "See, that man is blind; that dog is helping him." Comments such as these, by parents to their children, mark both the beginning and the perpetuation of the banal courtesies that characterize the interpersonal commerce of the customary face-to-face of disability and nondisability. Turning to the Other, what Levinas refers to as the "inter-human recourse" that we have to one another for help, disabled people find a "face" but usually one "dimmed" with the conception of disability as misfortune. The trope that brings disability face-to-face with nondisability is framed within the ideological superiority of the latter and is thus "seen" as a "cry for help." The appearance of disabled people in the public realm is directed by this framing, and thus interaction between disabled and nondisabled people is often animated by an obligation to "help the unfortunate."

The relationship between disability and nondisability depends not only on the two categories' being understood as binary opposites but also on the body's being conceived of as "natural," as "given." But, as Judith Shklar (1990, 5) says, "We must recognize that the line of separation between injustice and misfortune is a political choice, not a simple rule that can be taken as a given." The line that separates disability from nondisability is understood as a given, drawn once and traced over and over again with the indelible pencil of nature. The scenography of human life is sketched with this imagined pencil of nature, marking a complex network of distinctions between what we choose and what is a given. But these lines of demarcation, as Frank (1998, 209) suggests, are "blurred" (in flux) and remain so, despite the continuous tracing. Ironically, it is the blurriness of these lines of demarcation that calls for such continuous tracing.

Humanity is constantly involved in this act of demarcation; we trace lines, for example, between nature (what is given to us) and nurture (what we make of what is given to us), contextualizing human life by making distinctions also between nature and society, sex and gender, health and illness, disability and nondisability. Human life is played out in the scene of this network of distinctions. Our treatment of one another is enmeshed in this complex network. Complex as this network is, however, the "rule of the given" of which Shklar speaks clarifies any "blurriness" between misfortune and injustice and prevents any recognition of the politics (choice) of such a distinction. This results in the "pencil of nature" being equated with the "pencil of normalcy"; thus, able-bodiedness is "natural/normal," disability is not. Neither is political, since the one is nature, the other is "nature gone wrong." There is nothing just or unjust here, there is merely nature and misfortune. This presupposition of the "body as nature" grounds the "naturalness" of thinking of, and even experiencing, disability as "misfortune." "To call a presupposition into question is not the same as doing away with it; rather, it is to free it from its metaphysical lodgings in order to understand what political interests were secured in and by that metaphysical placing, and thereby to permit the term to occupy and to serve very different political aims" (Butler 1993, 30).

The presupposition that the matter (materiality) of the body, either the disabled one or the nondisabled one, is nature—the one normal, the other not—is itself not made by the "matter-of-nature." That the body can be spoken of as "natural" and that disability can be "prefigured" by impairment, also thought of as "natural," does not mean that these distinctions need necessarily be treated as a "given" and, therefore, as a "rule." To do so, presupposes a politics of the body and is thus to invoke a language in which is embedded a hegemonic ideology of an either/or dichotomy recommending that you either have a "normal body" or you do not. This hegemonic ideology remains "lodged" in the perpetuation of this dichotomy for, as Butler (1993, 35) suggests, "When this material effect is taken as an epistemological point of departure, a *sine qua non* of some political argumentation, this is a move of empiricist foundationalism that, in accepting this constitutive effect as a primary given, successfully buries and masks the genealogy of power relations by which it is constituted." The constitutive power relations of disability resides in what I call "useless-difference." Thus, disability does not, and should not, make a difference in the world. The idea of useless-difference suggests that disability makes a difference only to the individual and it does so in two important ways: it engenders "suffering" in the other and it has a psychological effect. The individual who now finds himself or herself disabled, or the one who is born so, will be traumatized to some degree and will now have to "accept" the disability, "cope" with it, and "adjust" to it. This difference, in its twofold character, is useless insofar as it is "passive," to borrow from Levinas, and inserts nothing essentially different into the world. Everything remains the same—the world still sees, despite blindness; the world still hears, despite deafness; the world still has places accessed only by stairs, despite people in wheelchairs; and parents still count the fingers and toes of their newborn. Blindness, deafness, and paraplegia are still unfortunate conditions that some of us have to suffer and are not (yet?) worthwhile and legitimate alternatives. They are not alternative ways of sensing the world and moving through it. Thus, disability becomes a difference that should be prevented, not "lived-in." We should see clouds for what they are, posts and people; we should not live in clouds, let alone be intrigued by their mystery. The political aim of privileging normalcy, expressed in the language of the body as natural and conditional, is what lies buried beneath and is masked by the empirical distinction between disability and nondisability.

This distinction, which renders disability as useless-difference and as a personal problem burdensome to both the individual and society, commingles with a specific version of "help." It expresses itself in the "inter-personal commerce" of which Levinas speaks and can be found in the banalized courtesies and customs that often mark the interaction between disabled and nondisabled people in contemporary society. But, the useless-difference of disability can also derive an extreme version of help that goes far beyond this customary courtesy even though it is equally banalized. I end this chapter with a brief example of such "help," which springs from the "natural" sense that clouds are indeed not clouds—that freedom is not disability.

Tracy Latimer: Our Problem

On October 24, 1993, Robert Latimer, a Saskatchewan farmer, killed his twelve-year-old daughter, Tracy.[8] Tracy was born with cerebral palsy and as she grew older, Tracy experienced physical pain, described as severe by her parents as well as by physicians. Tracy had surgery to correct the abnormal formation of her hips and to alleviate some of her pain. Her father, no longer able to witness the pain of his daughter, or so his defense lawyer claimed, killed her.

Robert Latimer confesses: "I took her in the truck, took her to the shed, closed both doors, hooked up a hose to the exhaust pipe and put it in the cab" (Eckstein 1995, 6). Tracy died of carbon monoxide poisoning. This was not the first time that Latimer thought of killing his daughter: "I don't know what day it was. I was combining. I thought I'd give her some Valium. . . . I was going to shoot her in the head and burn her in a fire" (6).

This time, however, Latimer did not merely think of killing Tracy, he actually did. Tracy's pain was too much for him. For Latimer, killing her was an "act of mercy" and not a criminal act. In a CBC interview, Latimer said, "I honestly don't believe there was ever any crime committed here" (6). Responding to the Court after his second-degree murder conviction, Latimer said, "I still feel I did what was right" (6).

As can be expected, the Latimer case has been embroiled in legal appeals. In 1994, Robert Latimer was convicted of second-degree murder and was sentenced to life imprisonment with no parole for a minimum of ten years. The conviction was appealed in 1995 and the 1994 decision was upheld. Another appeal granted Latimer a new trial and in 1997 he was retried. He was once again convicted of second-degree murder but with a new twist; Latimer's sentence of life imprisonment with no parole for a minimum of ten years was reduced to two years, only one of which had to be served in a prison. In an unprecedented action, the judge invoked Latimer's constitutional rights under the Canadian Charter of Rights and Freedoms and ruled that the ten-year minimum sentence was "cruel and unusual punishment." This decision was overturned by the Supreme Court of Canada and the initial sentence of a minimum of ten years in prison was upheld early in 2001.

The rationale for Latimer's appeals was that his killing of his daughter was an "act of mercy." The court, the media, and physicians, as well as Tracy's parents described her cerebral palsy as a "severe disability" causing Tracy to experience "severe pain" (Enns 1999, 9–47). The media depicted Tracy not only as suffering from severe pain but also as "helpless" both physically and mentally. Thus, her father was behaving "mercifully" when he killed her and life imprisonment with no parole for a minimum of ten years was seen as cruel and unusual punishment. The idea that he behaved "mercifully" represented the whole of Latimer's defense in court and represented, in part, the grounds of his appeal. This aspect of the appellant's factum reads as follows: "Trial judge erred . . . in not charging the jury that they could find that Robert William Latimer had the legal right to decide to commit suicide for his daughter, by virtue of her complete absence of physical and intellectual abilities . . . judge erred in law in not holding that the minimum sentence for murder on the facts of this case is a cruel and unusual punishment, contrary to S.12 of the Charter" (Eckstein 1995, 1).

Latimer was certainly not alone in his understanding that killing his daughter was necessary and that it was an act of mercy. In fact, Latimer has received wide support for both his action and his appeal. In a May 1999 CTV, News 1 interview, Latimer said, "One of the most important things to mention is all the people all across the country that have sent some really good letters and things like that, and over 175,000 to try and beat the government off on this one, . . . they are powerful letters. There's a professor from Saskatoon who said he was ashamed to be a Canadian when the first verdict was announced" (*Canadian News Bulletins,* May 6, 1999).

I want, finally, to speak of what Laura Latimer, Tracy's mother, thought of her daughter's murder. Laura Latimer and Tracy's siblings were at church at the time of Tracy's murder. Here is a portion of how Laura Latimer responded to defense questioning during her husband's trial.

> *Defense lawyer:* As Tracy developed in her first year, was there any suggestion that Tracy would not live at home?
> *Laura Latimer:* No. — when she was born? No.
> *Defense lawyer:* What were your hopes for her at that stage?
> *Laura Latimer:* When we very first took Tracy home we knew that she had brain damage but they said it might be very mild or it might be worse. We . . . had every hopes that . . . she would be

able to go to school but would just be maybe slow in school. . . .
We tried to treat her like a normal child . . . we tried to make her
life as normal as we could."

Defense lawyer: "How did you feel after Tracy died?

Laura Latimer: When I found Tracy I was happy for her . . . I was
happy because she didn't have to deal with her pain anymore.
After she died . . . I don't even know if I cried. Tracy's her birth
was way, way sadder than her death . . . we lost Tracy when she
was born and . . . that's when I grieved for her . . . I did all my
grieving when she was little. We lost her then. (Quoted in
Eckstein 1995, 6–7)

After killing his daughter, Robert Latimer removed her body from the
truck and placed it back in bed. This is where Laura Latimer, return-
ing from church, found Tracy and "discovered" that she was dead.

Latimer was faced with a daughter whom he "saw" as suffering from
a severe disability and from severe pain. Despite the fact that he with-
held pain medication from Tracy and one surgical procedure for her
and despite the fact that he refused a permanent replacement home
for Tracy (Eckstein 1995), he killed her because the pain was too much
for him; he decided to put Tracy "out of her misery" and to perform
the ultimate act of mercy. But, as Cheryl Eckstein (1995, 1) asks, "And
whose pain are we really talking about?"

Clearly, Tracy was not the only one suffering from severe pain. This
point brings us back to Levinas and "useless-suffering." Latimer was
suffering and the source of his suffering was Tracy's suffering; he was,
as Levinas puts it, suffering suffering. To him, Tracy's disability was
nothing other than the moans, groans, and sighs of suffering of which
Levinas speaks. Tracy's disability was "heard" (interpreted by Latimer) as a "cry for help" and he responded by silencing her cry once
and for all.

Extreme as it is, death is the practical consequence of Latimer's version of "help." In the face of suffering, Latimer responds with help and
this "help" takes the form of eliminating the suffering. And by eliminating Tracy's suffering, he eliminated his own suffering as well. The
elimination of one is simultaneously the elimination of the other. It is
useless to suffer the suffering of another when both can be eliminated.

Contrary to all opinion about the Latimer case—that of the media, of the courts, and of Latimer himself—his problem is not born of suffering. Latimer "knows" suffering all too well and he can recognize it when he "sees it." For him, no mistake, Tracy was suffering. Latimer was equally firm in his knowledge of what to do about suffering—eliminate it. For him, "do the right thing," eliminate Tracy's suffering through the only available means—eliminate Tracy. Latimer had resolved the question of suffering, and what to do about it, long before Tracy's birth. The only dilemma Latimer faced for years before the murder was whether to do it now or put it off. He was not vexed by Tolstoy's question, about how to live or by the question of what counts as life presupposed by this question. Latimer's resolution of such questions was both expressed and affirmed in his "practical ethics," which called for nothing other than the elimination of suffering.

Even though the professor from Saskatoon, and others, support Latimer's decision to eliminate his daughter's suffering and his own suffering of her suffering, how are disabled people to interpret these "practical ethics"? Ruth Enns (1999, 26) wonders, "If the facts could clearly establish the guilt of a murderer but the victim's disabilities could cloud the judgement of the media, the public and those representing the law, where could disabled people turn for protection and justice?"

In the face of disability, as I show in a previous discussion, suffering finds its place within a "seeing" that depicts disability as useless-difference. The appearance of blindness in the world, for example, is signified as the useless-difference of "abnormalcy," "defect," and "distortion," and thus is a difference that makes no difference to the "normal perception" of the world. But because blindness contributes nothing to "normal perception" does not mean that it is a "neutral" difference. After all, blindness contributes a great deal to the conventional understanding of the "normalcy of normal perception," according to which blindness is the sheer negation of sight and thus the opposite of all that is signified by sight—normalcy, knowledge, accuracy of perception. These qualities (and many others like them) are far removed from any empirical account or descriptive fidelity regarding the sense of sight. The same is true for blindness insofar as it does not empirically represent the lack of such qualities. It is not an "either/or" issue (Butler 1993, 254), specifying that either you can see and, therefore, have knowledge and accurate perception or you are blind and you do not. This either/or reasoning is borne of the understanding that sight and blindness are opposites and that they are opposed to one another in terms of these qualities. When qualities such as knowledge and accurate perception are connected to Enlightenment versions of empiricism, rationality, and reality, it is an almost imperceptible move to conceive of sight as a "powerful sense" and of blindness as the negation of such power. Far from being self-evident, therefore, the oppositional relation between sight and blindness is steeped within the power relations at play within the ideological struggle over what counts as reality and what counts as "seeing" and "knowing" it.

This rationality of opposites often governs conceptions and evaluations of the lives of disabled people. Thought of as the opposite of able-bodiedness, disability, and the lives of its people, is judged second-rate at best and unworthy at worst. This is the sort of "best of times and worst of times" sentiment that Tracy Latimer's mother, Laura Latimer, expressed during her husband's trial. Second-rate was the best that Laura Latimer could "see" in her daughter who had "brain damage" and there was the "hope" that Tracy would stay home and go to school even though a "little slow" in school was the best that could be expected. As she said, Laura Latimer "tried" to treat Tracy "like a normal child" and she and her husband "tried to make her life as normal as we could." Some semblance of normalcy was the best that could be hoped for, for a brain-damaged child. Expressions such as "normal treatment" and "normal as we could" are intelligible and even understandable when spoken of an "abnormal" (brain-damaged) child but not so intelligible and understandable when spoken of a "normal" child. Hopes and desires for "normalcy" are spoken and heard only within a context that signifies "abnormalcy." Without such a context, it is difficult to imagine Laura Latimer expressing these hopes for her "normal" (non-brain-damaged) children or to imagine any parent expressing any such hopes. Either a child is "abnormal" and must be "treated as normal" or a child is "normal" and no such "treatment" is necessary.

Tracy's mother "lost her" when she was born not only with "brain damage" but also with "normalcy damage." There was no need for tears when Laura Latimer found her daughter, dead, in her bed where Robert Latimer placed her after killing her. When she "found" her daughter's body, Tracy's mother was "happy for her." She was happy "because she [Tracy] didn't have to deal with her pain any more." Crying was unnecessary because Tracy's birth "was way sadder than her death." "We lost Tracy when she was born"; for Laura Latimer, that was the time for grieving. All grieving for Tracy was done when she was "little"; "we lost her then."

Laura Latimer's account involves at least two versions of "loss." There was, of course, the loss of her twelve-year-old daughter: Tracy was killed. But this loss did not necessarily call for grieving because Tracy was always-already lost to her parents. Tracy was dead from the moment she was born. Unlike the other Latimer children, Tracy was born without the prerequisite condition of normalcy (nondamaged brain). What is more, Tracy was born with the condition of physical pain—again not, for the Latimers, a prerequisite condition of normalcy. This was barely the birth of a human, let alone a normal, child.

There was no celebration of Tracy's birth; there were only tears, only grieving; they "lost her then." Tracy's birth held no promise for the Latimers. This brain-damaged infant the Latimers called Tracy would never develop into a normal child, a normal adolescent and would certainly never achieve even a semblance of what the Latimers conceived of as independence or adulthood. All of this—life—was lost to the Latimers "back then," when Tracy was born.

What was lost to the Latimers was personhood; Tracy's birth did not manifest any precondition for such a status and thus personhood was an impossibility. The Latimers saw no condition that would allow them to see her as cerebral palsy, or as a disabled child; they did not even see her as a child with a disability. Since personhood was impossible for Tracy, so was "seeing" her as a person with a disability. As the Latimers' "scene of life" spread out before them, they saw no frame for the possibility of the lived experience of cerebral palsy. There were only "persons with ——" in the Latimers' scene of life and since Tracy was born without the preconditions for "person," the Latimers could not see Tracy in their scene. "I believe that the term 'person with a disability' demonstrates and is underscored by a 'normative' resemblance that we [disabled people] can attain if we achieve the status of being deemed 'people first' (with the term's emphasis on independence and extreme liberal individualism) in the eyes of an ableist-centred society" (Overboe 1999, 24). Thus, we accept "the great equalizer—normality, the bench mark for humanity" (24). Despite losing Tracy at birth, Laura Latimer did see the possibility of Tracy's resembling normalcy. The possibility was slim, however, and Tracy would be "slow," at best, in school. Her parents would treat Tracy as "normal" as possible, as normal as one could treat a "brain-damaged" child. This was the best that could be "hoped" for her. But that "great equalizer—normality" was only a hope for the Latimers. The loss of normalcy and personhood—the loss of Tracy—occurred at her birth and her actual death was inevitable and anticlimactic. Robert Latimer killed his *already dead* daughter. As he said, no crime was committed; he did the right thing.

Robert Latimer's act of murder reflects the view that normalcy is the bench-mark for measuring humanity. To be human is to be normal, average, and just like everyone else; it is to be without the requirement of "normal treatment." "Normal treatment" is restricted to those who, although they are like everyone else, have a useless-difference. Privileging personhood and devaluing the lived experience of disability (Overboe 1999) is the register known as "normal treatment." The Latimers could not conceive of Tracy as a "person with a disability" since they could not see any person in her. They could see only disability (cerebral palsy and physical pain) in Tracy and this was death for the Latimers, not merely the reminder of it (Davis 1997, 1) but death itself. The Latimers could not conceive of the possibility of living disability and since it was impossible for Tracy to be a "person with a disability" it was equally impossible for Tracy to be.

The case of Tracy Latimer involves far more than the life and death of a child and whether a parent, the courts, or practical ethicists can and should decide when an "extreme case of disability" is too extreme. Tracy Latimer is a problem for all of us. She reminds us of what we all face when, at birth, we are inserted into ready-made social identities. What is given to us when we are given birth? What is given when disability is given birth? What choices (politics) are involved in the "birthing of disability"? What politics places disability on one side or the other of the line between misfortune and injustice?

5

The Birth of Disability

A s often as I have celebrated the day of my birth, I have never celebrated the birthday of my blindness. No societal convention exists that provides for the celebration of the acquisition of a disability or even for any exact designation of a day on which it was acquired and, furthermore, rarely can such a day be firmly established in the actual experience of acquiring a disability.

I do, for example, remember quite vividly the experience of not seeing the line-drive but I do not recall the exact day on which it occurred. The best I can do is recall how old I was at the time, through a process of deduction, using age markers, such as the school grade I was in at the time and the age eligibility for playing Little League baseball. Still, even these recollections, whether my own or those of my parents, do not tell me enough to establish the exact day on which I "lost" that line-drive.

There is something even more crucial involved in all of this: even if the exact day on which I did not see that line-drive could be established, would that be the birthday of my disability? Or, would the birth of my disability be marked by a later date—the day I could not see the blackboard, for example? Perhaps the date was even later than that.

I do remember, again quite vividly, my first visit with an ophthalmologist. How soon after not seeing the line-drive or the blackboard
this visit occurred, however, I do not know. All I remember is going to
the ophthalmologist with my parents and going with some expectation
of getting the "problem fixed."

My parents were in the examination room with me when the ophthalmologist began by asking me to read the letters on the Snellen
chart. I was familiar with this chart because a nurse had come to school
and had put all of the students through the test. I did not remember
much about it except that it was kind of fun to read all of the letters
the nurse pointed to on the chart. It seemed to me to be some sort of
accomplishment then. But this time, try as I might, I could not read
any of the letters to which the ophthalmologist was pointing. I knew
that there were letters on the chart but all I could see were smudges.
These, I knew, were letters, but I could not see them. The next thing
the ophthalmologist did was to look into my eyes with, what I came to
know several ophthalmological examinations later, as an ophthalmoscope. It was a bizarre experience. The ophthalmologist shut the lights
in the examination room and brought this instrument, which looked
like a pen with a bright light at its tip, very close to my eyes. His face
was just as close since he held his eye tightly against the instrument,
which, in turn, was not more than an inch away from my eyes or so it
seemed. I have had scores of such examinations since and I still experience the same sense of bizarreness. The ophthalmologist is so
close—his touch, the sound of his breathing, his muffled instructions
to look up, look down, look left, look right, even his smell—all of this,
so close, so intimate but so invasive, all of this, into my eyes. It was as
though the ophthalmologist entered my eyes and had a look around. I
could not do this; all I saw from the inside out was a bright light, nothing else; he looked inside—in the left side of my eye, the right, the top,
the bottom—he looked all around and took his time doing it. He saw
a lot more from the outside in than I did from the inside out, presumably. He made sounds as he looked around, sounds that were both
bizarre and frightening to me at the time. He cleared his throat and ut-
tered several "ahems" and many "hems." I came to know these sounds

as characteristic of those who looked in and around my eyes; all ophthalmologists make them. Muted as these sounds are, they are not inarticulate (Frank 1995, 27). They are the expressions of the one who is looking in and around something very interesting, something very extraordinary, and something very puzzling.

After the examination with the ophthalmoscope, the ophthalmologist leaned back and said something, something, extraordinary as it seems, that has been repeated almost word for word by most ophthalmologists who have subsequently conducted such an examination "in my eyes." Even though my parents and I were in the examination room, what the ophthalmologist said when he leaned back did not seem to be spoken to any of us. He spoke as if to no other person in the room but himself. The words he spoke, words I have come to hear over the years as an ophthalmological refrain, were "It's messy in there."

Over the years, I developed a response refrain, but on only one occasion did I ever speak it aloud. Whenever I hear, "It's messy in there," I think, "You should see it from this side." On the one occasion I did speak this refrain aloud and directly to the ophthalmologist, his response was not what I expected. He maintained his serious demeanor; he did not laugh or comment; he merely paused briefly and began making notes in a file. Either he thought I was making a joke about my eyesight and did not think it appropriate to join in or he thought I was making light of his comment, or even of ophthalmology, and did not find it funny. Either way, it was clear to me that the messiness in my eyes was to be seen only from the outside in and that it was no joking matter. The ophthalmological refrain has been repeated to me several times since, and even though my response comes to mind each time, I have never spoken it aloud again.

Immediately after saying, "It's messy in there," to no one in particular, the ophthalmologist turned to my parents and said, "He's blind." What in particular my mother said, I do not recall but I do remember her questioning him. The ophthalmologist explained, still facing my parents, that I was blind because I could not see the big E on the Snellen chart. I suspect that the ophthalmologist said other things to my parents, but I do not remember. Vivid in memory, however, is being presented with the ophthalmological fact that I was blind because I could not see the big E. And yet, I do not recall the exact day of this authoritative pronouncement and, more important, I do not think of this day as the first day of my blindness.

But was there ever such a day? Is it possible for me and for others to know the day that marks the birth of our disabilities in the same way that we can be precise about our birthdays? Margrit Shildrick and Janet Price (1996, 93) see disability as a "set of conditions" marked by the feature of fluidity. As a fluid and shifting set of conditions, disability cannot be categorically defined, nor can the actual acquisition of a disability. Even though the acquisition date of an impairment may be known, this is not a sufficient condition for disability since it ignores the fluidity of disability and thus fixes it in a once-and-for-all category. I passed as fully sighted during my teens; I stopped passing in my twenties; I began writing about disability in my late twenties. Does each of these represent the same disability or does each represent the acquisition of a new disability? Each does represent a different relation to disability. Seeing disability as a fluid and shifting set of conditions permits us, both individually and collectively, to experience multiple births of even a singular disability and thus allow us to experience the manyness of disability.

What, Not Who

"I'm what?" This response is what flooded my mind and, as I remember it, my entire body when I heard the ophthalmologist tell my parents that I was blind because I could not see the big E. After all, I could see, perhaps not baseballs or blackboards, but I could see. It was not until my early teens that I learned, from another ophthalmologist, who first repeated the "messy" refrain, that blindness means 10 percent vision or less. He said that I had no more than 10 percent vision and that my visual acuity was 20/200. I did not understand the meaning of what he said till much later.

What I was when I left the ophthalmologist's office with my parents that day was blind. Yet, I was blind and not blind; I could not see the big E, so I was, but I could see, so I was not. Overhearing my grandmother speaking of diminishing eyesight and hearing it as a sure sign of imminent death, I thought I might be dying prematurely, but I was not blind. This sensibility stayed with me even after the ophthalmologist told me that blindness means 10 percent or less of normal vision. It was not as though I disputed what the ophthalmologist told me, I just did not experience it. I was diagnosed as having macular degeneration. Later, the diagnosis was retinitis pigmatosa, and still later, it reverted to macular degeneration. This shift in ophthalmological diagnosis continues to this day.

But now, I had two things; I had a definition of blindness and a diagnosed, legitimate eye condition that reached far beyond not seeing the big E. Now I had something and what I had was blindness. Even though it may have been what I was, blind was not who I was. My blindness was not a fluid and shifting set of conditions. It was a singularly fixed and external condition, one ophthalmologically diagnosed as such. For a long time, my parents took me from one ophthalmologist to another to find out whether "anything could be done" about this condition I had. When I was older, I took myself to several more and with the same goal in mind. I do not recall exactly when I stopped this "ophthalmologist hopping" but it was certainly before the appointment I had in my early twenties with the genetic ophthalmologist. Even though I still had around 10 percent vision when I stopped this ophthalmologist hopping, this moment did mark yet another birth of yet another one of my blindnesses. It remained an external condition and what I was, but it shifted from a condition of which I could perhaps rid myself to one that would remain attached to my self forever. As firmly attached as this "thing" was to me, it certainly was not me.

Recall that during my teens I tried especially hard to cover up this thing called blindness that attached itself so firmly to me. I covered it with a panoply of interactions that effectively kept it out of the view of others. With a history of experience with, and belief in, the natural body (naturally seeing eyes), I tried, although I was less effective, to keep it out of my view as well. Because my family and I moved to a large city shortly after I began experiencing diminishing sight, by the time I was in high school, only I, my family members, those I knew back in childhood, and one or two teachers, could "see" that I had blindness.

There is no doubt that blindness was born, and born more than once, during my childhood and adolescence. But it was not I who gave birth to it; instead, it was some version of the "natural" cloaked in ophthalmological practices that brought my blindness to life. I was genetically predisposed, as it turned out, to "getting" blindness. It lurked somewhere in my genes for about eleven years or so before it made an appearance and attached itself to me more firmly.

Staging a Self

In what follows I show how disability involves a staging of the self, a disciplinary practice of the body, and the contesting of an identity bound within a minimalistic view of disability. According to Margrit Shildrick and Janet Price (1996, 93–94): "It is not that we want to advocate a social construction model of disability, but rather to ask: How do disabilities mediate the staging of the self? How does the label constitute a disciplinary practice of the body? And how in particular does ME [myalgic encephalmyelitis] contest those fantasies of control by which we seek to secure our bounded identities?"

During my adolescence, the only self that I was interested in staging was my "sighted self." This self was born of my childhood where I became tightly connected to a history and an identity with and in the "world of the normal." My identity was firmly lodged in an ubiquitous sensibility of the "natural body." Although I achieved a fully sighted self through interaction (by passing), my commitment to this self was virtually no different from those who were fully sighted. They too were required to stage a sighted self and, like me, they did so through interaction that revealed them to be sighted both to others and to themselves, a process Harold Garfinkel (1967, 1) calls "accountability." Sighted people have to act as though they can see in order to be seen as seeing; they need to make eye contact, notice one another, move around things *because* they *see* them; they, as Milligan says, "live in their eyes" (Magee and Milligan 1995, 45).

I was no different; I too "lived in my eyes." I acted and interacted "as if" I were as fully sighted as everyone else. I made eye contact; I maneuvered around obstacles in the streets; I crossed traffic-light-controlled intersections. But where I was different from others lay in the fact that my acting "as if" was genuine insofar as I was constantly aware of my "as if" status as a sighted self. Not being able to see the traffic lights at an intersection, for example, I needed to "check out" vehicular and pedestrian traffic flow in order to determine whether the light was in my favor, and I needed to accomplish this "as if" I were not doing so. I did the same with eye contact. My central vision contains, what seems to me, a tight circle of ever-moving colored lights. I need to look around these lights in order to see. Doing so while making eye contact, however, means that I would be looking past a person's eyes and not in them. I learned how to quickly focus this tightly bound circle of colored lights on a person's face. This is my version of making eye contact. For me, not seeing a face or eyes translated into "making eye contact."

My sighted self, the self I presented to the world was not staged in the Goffmanesque sense that provides for the possibility of disingenuousness. I was genuinely sighted—I "lived in my eyes." Still, I knew I was legally blind. I did not doubt this existential fact during my adolescence. But, "this legal blindness" was not me; it was something that attached itself to me with a firm grip. The most sophisticated ophthalmological practices proved not nearly strong enough to loosen its grip and tear it from me.

The tighter the grip of blindness became, the more ferociously I clung to my sighted self. This process began quite innocently in childhood. Soon after I "lost" that line-drive, I began experiencing (seeing) the tightly wound circle of lights. It was very small back then, compared with what it is now. Now, almost my entire visual field is made up of shimmering colored lights. Back then, the circle seemed like a speck. I began rubbing my eyes in an attempt to remove it. Despite the futility of this action, I continued this practice for quite some time. Even now, I occasionally rub these colored lights. Back then, however, it seemed as though these colored lights should be something that could be rubbed away. I knew that this speck of colored lights was somehow in me, but I experienced (saw) it as something I was "looking at." Like anything else I was looking at, it should have disappeared when I looked away from it or rubbed it out. Rubbing did not work and anywhere I looked that little speck of colored lights was there. It turns out that the biomedical model of the body, including eyesight, was as tightly wound in me as was that speck of colored lights.

The culture of science as a dominant ideology of both knowledge and knowing was part of me even in childhood. Together with my family and ophthalmologists, I saw that ever-growing speck of colored lights through the lens of science, in particular that of ophthalmological science. I knew that there was something wrong with my eyes and I knew, too, that eye specialists, as I called them at that time, were the ones who knew how to fix the problem. I also knew what it was like to see without colored lights and I knew that the former was the right way and the latter the wrong. There was something wrong with my eyes, and even my grandmother said that diminishing sight was a sign that death was not far away. Primitive as it was, I was already beginning, as a ten- or eleven-year-old child, to develop a sense of the "natural body." Undoubtedly, the predominance of science in school together with folklore such as that of my grandmother's was working in combination with ophthalmological visits, and I was well on my way to embodying my self in the "natural body."

The expansion of the circle of colored lights only substantiated this sensibility. What came through the lights was the immutable fact that the natural body (seeing normally) was the "right" body and that the natural body gone "wrong" (not seeing normally) was the "wrong" body. For a very long time my colored lights mediated the self I staged, in the sense Shildrick and Price suggest, by instilling in me an unshakeable commitment to the natural body.

I found this same sense of the natural body in relation to seeing in the parents of a blind child. In an interview with me, the father reported what the pediatric ophthalmologist told him immediately after his son was diagnosed as "legally blind" at three months of age: "He told me to go out and buy a telescopic lens from a telescope and give him that to play with. So he can learn, like if we teach him to play with it at an early age, he'd get used to it" (Father 2000). These parents said that more than one ophthalmologist had told them that this diagnosis was not temporary and that their son would grow up legally blind. They agreed with the advice they were given about the lens. Since their son would be legally blind all of his life, getting used to this kind of device, they thought, was a good idea. But there was something else their son was getting used to; at a very young age, he was already being shown that his "way of seeing" was not normal. Further, technology was becoming a part of his life at a very early age. The "problem of blindness" was already being formulated for this three-month-old; he was to understand that blindness is a technical problem requiring technical solutions. While this conception of blindness is undoubtedly true on some level, it does restrict the imaginary of blindness to the realm of the technical. The child was getting used to it and thus to his version of self. The child's playing with a telescope—all that a three-month-old can do with such an instrument—recalls George Herbert Mead's interpretation (1934, 365) of "play" as a precursor to a child's development of a sense of the "generalized other." The generalized other in this case is signified by "normal vision." Furthermore, playing with a telescope in infancy may signify that a legally blind child can only play at seeing since really seeing is out of the question. Technical problem aside, it remains to be "seen" whether or not "playing at seeing" is a bad thing for this three-month-old or for the rest of us.

Disability and the Constitution of a Disciplinary Practice of the Body

I recently interviewed "Don," a fourth-year university student. Don is, in his words, a "total blindie" and has been so since infancy. He attends a large university in a large city and, to help him get around, uses a white cane, which he interchangeably refers to as "my stick" and "crowd control."

You find yourself doing a lot more eavesdropping than sighties do. Then you learn, hear, all sorts of good stories. . . . Well, because you can't look around at the people. Most sighties, you know, they'll look at someone and they figure they know about the person by looking at them. But when you can't look at 'em that isn't the case. The only way you're going to learn much about 'em is to listen to all their secret stories . . . then you probably know 'em better than someone looking at 'em. . . . If you sit next to someone on a bus, you kinda brush up against them and then if you notice if they're slouching, well, then they're in a bad mood. But sighties want to help you on a bus 'cause they think blindies can't do anything. They grab you by the wrist when you're standing and you can't balance yourself on a bus when you're standing. . . .

One day, like I was a bit ripped still from the night before and my sense of balance wasn't back right. The bus came to this stop and I wanted to get off. I got up and the guy grabbed me, but he wouldn't get up. I assume he at least would have helped me find a door even though I knew damn well where the door was. I figured he figured I needed help to get there. So I started walking toward the door, [but] he wouldn't get up, [and] the bus was just about going to leave the stop, right? And I started walking and my feet were walking out from under me 'cause the top of me couldn't move. And, again my sense of balance was all screwed up, you know, I just about went over and smashed my head on the back of the seat. He got a good pile on the face out of it though. . . .

You see what it is, some, some blind people have, you know, enough skills to get around and other ones don't. What you fall into is that people see the blind people that don't have the skills and think you're—that's, normal, 'cause you know they think, well, they stand out, right. And so they're going to take that as being the general case. And it doesn't need to be. It probably is more than it needs to be, because a lot of blind people will fall for that trick.

Sometimes you get—, because sometimes when I'm walking down a sidewalk, right? It's a new route and I want to know what's up and down the sides of the sidewalk. You know, the middle's pretty boring. I want to know what's at both sides not just one side. I'll go over to one side, walk a ways and go to the other side and walk a ways. And it looks like I'm either drunk or wiped out or . . . you know, whatever. But it's only 'cause I want to know what the hell's there. And, the only way I can know that, is to go there. Going straight is, you know, a drag, 'cause you do that so much. (Don 2000)

Don does not remember ever seeing. He said: "That's what they called me; they called me blind since I can remember. I don't even know when I figured it out, you know, if you're blind, you're blind. That's all you know, so you figure . . . well, then you hear people say, 'I see this,' 'I see that,' and you think, '"See"? What's that?' Then you figure, well, it's something they got, I don't." Don clearly knows that, unlike him, people see. He is, however, not as clear about what seeing is other than that it is something that other people have and that he does not. Nor is he clear about when he came to understand himself as blind or how he came to understand blindness as not having sight. Don frames seeing within terms of mobility, as an ease and independence of bodily movement.

There is a definite sense in which Don experiences and conceptualizes both blindness and sightedness within a relationship between the body and the environment. A sense of distance emerges between the two, expressed as a finite distinction between people (subject) and the environment (object). Don recognizes this distinction in terms of what he has to do in order to be a perceiving subject and he frames it in terms of what sighted people do not have to do in order to be the same. Sighted people have the "thing" (sight) that allows them not to have to do what Don does in order to be a perceiving subject. Not having this thing (sight), Don has to do other things.

Seeing a new street is easy for sighted people; they need only "look around" and they can walk down the middle of the sidewalk while doing so. For sighted people, a new street is just that, while, for Don, a new street signifies a new "route." Like other blind people, Don must walk "straight" and do "so much of it." If he veers from his route, there is a chance that he will become disoriented. For example, he must walk straight and thus allow himself to meet curbs "head on" so that he can judge intersecting sidewalks and streets. Veering may put him off course.

Sighted people can "look around" as they walk down a sidewalk and can do so just by literally looking around. Don, however, must leave the middle of the sidewalk and walk on one side of it for a while and then on the other. Don "looks around" with his "stick."

But, "looking around" presents a hazard to Don, a hazard other than the one of becoming disoriented. He is concerned with what he might "look like" while he is "looking around." The "look of looking" is far different for Don than it is for someone who sees. After all, Don will be weaving down the sidewalk as he looks around and he might just "look" drunk or whatever. Because of his "looking around," which is to say, his blindness, he may appear not as a perceiving subject but as a subject not in control of his body.

Don articulates an unexplicated version of sight as the "distance sense" (Howes 1991; Michalko 1999). The distance between people (the subject) and the environment (the object) is radically closed through the sense of sight. Seeing the environment is a simple matter of using opened eyes, of looking at it. Don, however, must go to the environment in order to "see it." Looking at the environment means that Don must come in touch with it. Weaving down the sidewalk; touching now this side, now the other, this is how Don "looks around." Don is "in touch" with what everyone else "looks at." But, even this "looking" makes him "look" as though he is drunk, or "whatever." The more Don closes the gap between the subject (himself) and the object (environment), the more he "looks" as though he is not in control of his body.

This issue of control, however, is grounded directly, for Don, in the commingling of the body and knowledge. It may "look" as though Don is weaving down the sidewalk in a drunken state, "but it's only 'cause I wanna know what the hell's there." Don's weaving signifies his desire to know; and, "the only way I can know that is to go there." Don knows through his body and not through his eyes. This body-knowledge presupposes and depends upon another kind of knowing. Don knows that what he comes to know about his environment is based on body-knowledge. He can conceptualize a sidewalk without "going there" and touching it from side to side just as sighted people can conceptualize a sidewalk without seeing it. Both Don and sighted people know what is likely to be on either side of a sidewalk, but to know what is on a particular sidewalk, Don must "go and touch" and sighted people must "look and see."

To get to know people, Don uses a similar process. He listens and, as he says, he does a lot more "eavesdropping than sighties do" because he "can't look around" at the people. For Don, there is no question that, first, people are knowable and, second, they are such through looking; people know something about one another by looking at each other. Unlike people who are sighted, who assume that by looking at people they know about them, Don must listen to people's "secret stories." By listening, Don knows people better, he thinks, "than someone lookin' at 'em." But he cannot know people from a distance; he must be "close enough to hear," even close enough to touch. Not only must Don "go" to his physical environment in order to know but he must "go" to his social one as well. He must go close enough to people to hear them in order to know them. "You don't even know if they're there unless they say something or if you smack 'em with your stick or something." If Don can get close enough, he can learn things about people that sight could never give him. What is more, Don says, sighted people don't even know this.

Don also uses body-knowledge to know people. For example, getting on a bus, he "kinda brushes up against" someone and if he notices that the person is "slouching," he concludes that "they're in a bad mood." But his "kinda" brushing is intentional. "Kinda" refers to the explicit achievement of such brushing as accidental, and it is yet another way that Don closes the gap between himself and his environment. Much like knowing what is on both sides of the sidewalk, Don must "go" to the person in order to know his or her emotional state. Whether he is right or wrong about such states is as irrelevant as whether or not sighted people are right or wrong when they "look and see" a person's emotional state.

Underlying the distinction Don makes between the ways blind people and sighted people perceive and know their physical and their social environments is the assumption that all people (blind or sighted) can know their environments. To know his environment Don must address the problem of distance. He uses touch to close the gap between himself and his environment and he uses touch and hearing to close the gap between himself and another person or persons. To know what is on both sides of the sidewalk, for example, Don goes there and touches whatever is there with his "stick." Or, when he sits beside someone on a bus, he reads the person's mood by subtly brushing up against him or her. Here Don experiences his blindness as the need to close the distance between himself and the objective realm of emotional states he "knows" to exist. As he says later in the interview, "If you're gonna know 'em [people] you gotta get close enough first."

Don also has learned a version of his culture's conventional understanding of embodied emotion—emotions reveal themselves through the language of the body. He intentionally comes in touch with the body of another in order to read this language—slouching body, for example, equals bad mood. Sight, however, is the typical and "natural" solution to the problem of distance and the perception of emotions, forcing on blindness the necessity of finding different and interactionally "unnatural" solutions.

To perceive emotional states, however, Don must also be vigilant and flexible. "Sighties, you know, they can see someone from a far ways. Then, they see that their face looks pretty down and they can tell that the guy's sad or in a bad mood or something. But, I don't know this, right? Someone comes up to me and I say, 'Hey, how're you doing!' you know, real happy. Then, he says, 'My sister just died.' And I say, 'Oh, sorry.' You know, I gotta change real quick. Sighties don't need to do this."

Vigilance and flexibility are essential qualities when closeness is necessary. In brushing up against someone on a bus, Don does not want to reveal any intention; he wants the brushing to be perceived as innocent and unintended. He does the same when he eavesdrops as a way to get to know someone. Don must get close enough to reach his goal of getting to know someone but not so close as to reveal any intention, especially that of eavesdropping. Closing the distance between the perceiving subject and the perceivable object is tricky because it entails getting close enough and no closer. In these tricky situations, Don must be flexible enough, for example, to remedy an instance of "too close" if his brushing up is interpreted this way.

As objective as Don understands his environment to be, he does not think of it as static, and thus, here, too, he must be vigilant and flexible. As he says, "Things change, sighties move stuff around, you know, they can see, so what do they care. Snow, that's the biggie. When it snows, everything disappears." The environment changes and, once it does, it disappears. Sighties and snow, more than anything else, widen the gap between Don and his environment.

Having no memory of seeing, Don imagines what seeing is. He imagines that sight permits for immediate and accurate knowledge of another's emotional state. He "knows" that the body expresses emotions, and thus he imagines that sighted people can read the language of the body at a distance and know what another is feeling. But Don can know what another is feeling only when he gets close enough and by then sometimes it is too late. His enthusiastic greeting is met, for example, with the voice of another filled with sadness. Ever vigilant and always flexible, Don changes his voice to demonstrate both his ability to perceive and his capacity for empathy.

To Don, vigilance and flexibility are not qualities necessary for sighted people. While he concedes that blind people and sighted people share a common and objective environment, Don believes that they have different relationships with that environment. Unlike René Gadacz (1994, 5), who says, "Disability can be viewed as a relationship between a person with a physical or mental impairment and the social and physical environment around him or her," Don sees no distinction in this view of disability between disabled people and nondisabled ones. That disabled people have a relationship with the environment, does not distinguish them from non-disabled people since they too have such a relationship. For Don, the distinction lies in the content of the relationship itself (Michalko and Titchkosky 2001). In relating to their environment, sighted people cover distances with their sense of sight, while blind people use their distance senses of touch and hearing to relate to that very same environment. Thus, accessibility as an aspect of the relationship with the surrounding environment can never have the same cogency for nondisabled people as it has for disabled people. Sight, hearing, mobility, and other so-called abilities bring the surrounding environment to nondisabled people, making it their environment. The environment does not come to disabled people; we must go to it. We have a relationship with an environment, but it is their environment and not ours. Non-disabled peoples' access to the environment is assumed to be given by the givenness of "natural abilities." In contrast, disabled people must continuously find, not to mention fight for, paths of access to the environment. Any semblance of what might be described as our environment for disabled people must be gleaned from a relationship with it other than the "naturally given" one of nondisabled people. The issue of accessibility for disabled people presupposes a relationship to the environment that aims at "taking" it as our own. The visceral need to belong of which Cornel West (1995) speaks is born of the "our/their" relation to the giving and taking of the environment.

Still, there is a sense in which the environment comes to disabled people. The fact that much of society's artifice is inaccessible to disabled people gives us society's view that it is not prepared for us and that it does not intend to be so, at least not fully. There are also social identities that circulate in the environment, identities ready-made for us and that come to us through societal representations of disability. I next interrogate the achievement of a "disability identity" that is formed through the interaction of societal images of disability and disabled people. To develop this interrogation I make use of the work of Jacques Lacan (1968, 1977) and of Arthur Frank (1994) on "illness narrative," which reformulates Lacan.

A Minimalist Orientation to Disability

Despite a disabled body, a going to and taking of the environment presupposes ability, but not in the contemporary register that conceives of disability as "differently abled." The concept of differently abled imagines a physical and social environment that is inclusive of disabled people and that is ours and not just theirs. This concept reconstitutes Lacan's sense of the Real, giving it new significance and evoking what he calls the Imaginary (1968, 1977).

The Realness of blindness as not-seeing spills into the environment not in Lacan's sense of "infinite plentitude" but as "infinite lack." What is Real about blindness is the unimaginable access to the infinite plentitude of the Real of seeing. Identity is thus bound by the imagined impenetrability of a border between plentitude and lack. The crossing of such a border is always imagined as penetration. Wheelchair ramps, curb cuts, sound indicators on elevators—all signify the penetration of lack into the infinite plentitude of nondisability. Such accommodations do not necessarily represent the transformation of their environment into ours. Instead, they represent what is required to accommodate lack. Along with this requirement, such accommodations symbolize lack in the environment insofar as the materiality of an environment is required to change in order to accommodate those (disabled people) who are beyond its intentions and expectations (Michalko and Titchkosky 2001). The environment cannot imagine disability in any other way than the penetration of lack into the infinite plentitude of environmental intentionality.

It is not surprising, then, that accommodations for disabled people are given grudgingly and with a fight and are provided reluctantly under the yoke of some legislation. There are innumerable examples; I was recently involved with one. I attended a university meeting organized to discuss accommodation needs for disabled people. The university was in the initial planning stages for the construction of a new building. University administrators invited disabled faculty and students to attend a meeting with them together with the architects commissioned to design the building. There were two ways that accommodation was spoken of by the university administrator that were particularly relevant.

The administrator, who was also chairing the meeting, asked the disabled people who were present to inform the architects of their particular accommodation needs. This request framed disability and accommodation as individual issues. I made two points: legislated building codes already included the legal requirement to make buildings accessible to disabled people and, since these requirements were minimal, the university should hire an architect who specializes in accessibility and accommodation issues. The architects and the disabled people in the room agreed. The architects reiterated the minimalistic approach that building codes had toward accommodation and accessibility and pointed out that their firm routinely makes use of consultants to remedy this minimalistic approach and that the cost of these consultants is built into their fee.

The university administrator said that caution was required. The building that the university is planning to construct is a large sports and recreation center. The administrator said that he knew of other such buildings that went "overboard" on matters of accessibility and even made the coach's bench in the hockey arena wheelchair accessible. Clearly, this was excessive to him. The meeting ended in a typical administrative way—all of our comments were important and very much appreciated and, given the restrictions of budget, would be taken "under advisement."

The particular university administrator displayed what is a ubiquitous orientation toward disabilities: disability is an individual issue and accommodation is also an individual matter and it can be excessive. The new building was described by both the administrator and the architects as a "wellness center" and, during the meeting, the administrator asked those of us who were disabled to delineate the "wellness needs of persons with disabilities." He did not say whether he had asked nondisabled people to delineate their "wellness needs." Presumably, doing so was not necessary since any building, including wellness centers, implicitly intend nondisabled people to show up. Accessibility and accommodation issues are reserved only for those of us who are disabled. The new building is necessarily intended for nondisabled people but not disabled people. For us, accessibility is conceived of in minimalistic terms, and though exclusion is not the intention of minimalistic approaches to accessibility, those who take these approaches do see disability itself as minimalizing.

The university administrator represented this minimalistic view of both disability and the need for accommodation. It was excessive, he suggested, that a sports facility should include wheelchair ramps as a form of access to hockey coaches' and players' benches. For him, it was clear that wheelchair use would prohibit anyone from playing hockey and thus no one using a wheelchair would require access to players' benches. He extended this rationale to hockey coaches and was equally clear that no one in a wheelchair would coach hockey. Wheelchair use was minimalizing to the extent that its use clearly prevented anyone from participating in hockey as a player or as a coach. Thus, the administrator's logic provided for only minimal accommodation to the hockey facility. He said that the stands and washrooms would have to be made accessible to those using wheelchairs.

The administrator could imagine wheelchair users only as spectators in a hockey facility. The Realness, to return to Lacan, of wheelchair use in a hockey facility was "bound" to the role of spectator and no other version of participation could be imagined. If wheelchair users were to participate at all in this facility, they would do so as spectators only. This expectation mirrors the role generally assigned by society to wheelchair users, as well as to other disabled people and accounts for the minimalistic approach to accessibility and accommodation in legislated building codes.

This minimalizing orientation to disability does resonate with Lacan's sense of Real, not literally in his notion of the infantile, and simultaneously infinite, plenitude of infancy, but rather in the conception of the infinite lack (limit) of disability. Reflecting on the "illness narrative"[1] in Lacanian terms, Frank (1994, 9) writes:

> The adult experience of illness at first seems the antithesis of infantile plenitude, but illness does recapitulate a version of the Real. The ill person, like the infant, is tied most closely to embodiment, the body is fragmented, and the experience of embodiment exceeds language. . . . The chaotic narrative [the Real] is a return to the condition of being mute and thus a reassertion of the Real, though this Real is now past language rather than before it. When chaos does begin to speak, the speech is a step into another type of narrative. The chaos can be spoken about—as we speak *about* infantile plenitude—but the subject cannot speak *from the position of* chaos. The authentic speech of the chaotic narrative is the scream, and beyond that, only silence.

It is possible to draw an analogy to disability narrative from Frank's work on illness narrative. The experience of disability also seems antithetical to infantile plenitude and also recapitulates a version of the Real. Like the ill person and the infant, the disabled person is tied most closely to embodiment. The disabled body—in the Real—is experienced as fragmentation, as broken and even as damaged (Murphy 1987).

The Real, or, as Frank calls it, the "chaos narrative," is recapitulated in the experience of chaos with/of such a body. Elsewhere (Michalko 1998), I refer to this experience of chaos as the "something-wrong." Nancy Mairs experienced something-wrong long before she was diagnosed with multiple sclerosis and long before she was, in her words, a "cripple." She writes:

> There were other signs to be explained or ignored. The lobby of the building at the Harvard Law School where I worked as a technical editor was paved with slate, and I started catching my toe on the slight irregularities in the floor's surface. I dropped lighted cigarettes from my left hand, and after a stretch of typing or knitting, my left fingers became so rubbery that I could hardly control them. A mysterious vertigo, diagnosed by the doctor as an "inner ear infection" then going around, kept me in a whirl for three weeks and then vanished. (Mairs 1996, 20)

Here, the something-wrong is experienced in the chaos of the inexplicable and the mysterious. Mairs has all these experiences—tripping for no apparent reason, dropping cigarettes inexplicably, and feeling vertigo— in the chaos of the something-wrong. She feels the Real of disability in the stark inability that has taken control of her for some mysterious reason. An infantile lack pervades her body as forcefully as the understanding of this lack abandons it. The "whirl" of the supposed inner-ear infection dramatically depicts the Real of disability.

The experience of a fragmenting body does indeed exceed language and thus exceeds its expression. Mairs is now speaking from a position other than the something-wrong or the Real. She has broken the silence of her chaos insofar as she talks about it and her disability narrative, while inclusive of her chaotic Real, is not spoken from that position. If the authentic speech of the chaos illness narrative is the "scream," the authentic speech of the chaos disability narrative is bewilderment. There is nothing beyond bewilderment in the Real of disability, in its infantile lack. Any identification with disability is yet to be developed.

As Frank (1994, 10) suggests, "For Lacan identity is formed by the sedimentation of images, beginning with the mirror image and progressing through various ego ideals." These images represent the self, but are not the self "and their inadequacy invests them with a certain hostility." Still, replete with inadequacy, images "are all the self has with which to construct an identity for itself." In Lacan's words:

> We have only to understand the mirror stage *as an identification*, in the full sense that analysis gives to the term: namely, the transformation that takes place in the subject when he assumes an image—whose predestination to this phase-effect is sufficiently indicated by the use, in analytic theory, of the ancient term imago.
>
> This jubilant assumption of his specular image by the child at the *infans* stage, still sunk in his motor incapacity and nursling dependence, would seem to exhibit in an exemplary situation the symbolic matrix in which the *I* is precipitated in the primordial form, before it is objectified in the dialectic of identification with the other, and before language restores to it, in the universal, its function as subject. (Lacan 1977, 2)

A disability identification is, without question, wrapped in a multi-layered complex of images. The sources of these images are societal representations of disability in general and various collective images in particular. Images of disabled people as heroic or tragic or as requiring pity, help, and charity abound in our contemporary society. Particular images of disability flow from the modern idea of the "expert," from which flows images of disability steeped in an ideologically based version of knowledge about disability. Medicine, for example, advocates a biological interpretation that yields an image of disability as requiring prevention or cure; an image that sees no value in disability as a life worth living. Rehabilitation and special education insist on such ideological practices as acceptance and adjustment as rational responses to disability. These forms of scientific-rationalistic versions of disability reflexively provide for the more general societal image of disabled people as either heroic or tragic. The reflexive trope imagines disability as "happening" to people; some accept this fate, adjust to it, and heroically perform the activities of daily life, ordinary as these activities may be; others succumb to the tragedy of disability and do not adjust. When disability is imagined as a tragic misfortune thus yielding an image of it as an almost impenetrable obstacle to the living of a life, the only imaginable course of action is that of "overcoming." Thus, the tragic misfortune image of disability equals either the heroic overcoming of it or the tragedy of not doing so.

It is not surprising that metaphors such as "battling" or "fighting" are used to depict disability both individually and collectively. Perhaps the quintessential image of society's "fight" against disability is Jerry Lewis's "kids" and his telethon to raise funds for cystic fibrosis research. But, there is another version of fighting disability, and it pits person against disability. For example, here is what a blind person, Doug Parisian, says about such a fight.

> I still feel, at times, that I have to fight and fight and fight to prove things to myself and to others. This can lead to what I call overkill. I'll do things that I probably shouldn't try to do. I'll walk places on my own where I'd be smarter to take an arm. Sometimes I'll do things to the extreme. For example, this fall I insulated my house. After six months of riding transit buses searching for the best insulation system, I finally found one. The procedure I chose meant I had to run vertical steel straps every two feet around my house and then attach a foam board insulation. I did that rotten, tedious job myself using a simple stepladder, a concrete drill and a screwdriver. I'm sure I turned over eight hundred screws. I refused the help that people offered partly because I felt that they would think less of me if I couldn't do it. (Parisian 1981, 89)

The collective battle to prevent disability and the individual fight on the part of many disabled people to prove things to themselves and to others is an integral and ubiquitous aspect of contemporary society. As different as these battles are, they do have a common enemy—negative societal images of disability. Whether medically based or steeped in the pity of Jerry Lewis–style telethons, these prevention programs are oriented toward eliminating what are conceived of as the inherently negative features that disability forces on a life, be it collective or individual. A life according to this view cannot be imagined outside of the images of it circulating within a society. It is as though a disabled person is this image.

Parisian, for example, feels that he has to do extreme things—what he calls overkill—in order to prove to himself and to others that he can do things. He received his blindness into himself as helplessness and incompetence and embarked on a fight against such an image of who he essentially is. Even though he has an intuition that such a fight inevitably leads to such extreme endeavors as insulating a house, he nonetheless continues the fight even when he feels it would be better to "take an arm." But, since taking an arm may be interpreted as helplessness by others, he heroically goes it on his own. Taking an arm represents, for Parisian, the possibility that he may in fact be, according to the societal image, helpless.

A similar sentiment was expressed to me by the father of a one-year-old legally blind boy with partial sight. I asked the father whether he would ever call his son blind. "Never, no, absolutely never," he responded. "It's like he'd be blind then. I'd never call him that and I wouldn't let anyone else call him that, even his teachers and people like that" (Father 1999). This father may be experiencing what I experienced when the ophthalmologist told me that I was blind, except this father is experiencing it from the point of view of a parent who is sighted. Still, why call someone blind when he can see? But this is not the only concern showing through in this father's comments. The concern is also for the power of the word *blind*. This father is afraid that if his son is called blind he will become the word, the thing itself, blindness, and he will become all of that which his father imagines blindness to be.

Recall Don: "You see what it is, some, some blind people have, you know enough skills to get around and other ones don't. What you fall into is that people see the blind people that don't have the skills and think you're that's, normal, 'cause you know they think, well, they stand out, right? And so they're going to take that as being the general case. And it doesn't need to be. It probably is more than it needs to be, because a lot of blind people will fall for that trick." Ironically, Don suggests that blind people themselves contribute to negative societal images of blindness. He suggests that blind people without the skills (to get around) are more noticeable than those with such skills. Presumably, Don is saying that blind people without skills become lost and disoriented and that they look as though they are. This sort of disorientation, according to Don, is more noticeable and thus generates a generalization on the part of sighted people that blind people are disoriented and get lost. What is interesting is that Don suggests that blind people with the skills to get around do not need to "fall for that trick." In the face of the causal relationship he draws between blind people and negative stereotypes, Don suggests that there is a "trick" involved. The trickiness of the situation resides in the understanding that a blind person does not have to become the societal image of blindness. One thinks of oneself as an image only when one is tricked into doing so. Don is making implicit reference to the power of societal images and generalizations and to the difficulty of escaping such images. It is tricky for a blind person to be seen as a competent traveler when viewed through the lens of generalization.

All of these examples—Parisian, the father of the blind child, and Don—implicitly recommend a solution to the problem of becoming the negative societal image of blindness: fight this image by creating another one. Parisian fights the image by becoming involved in extreme activities (overkill); the father of the blind child intends always to avoid the word *blind* in relation to his son; and Don resists falling for the societal trick of generalization and stereotyping. Parisian and Don create the image of competence and skilled traveler, respectively. The father of the blind child fights societal images of blindness by avoiding the word altogether. All are steeped in what Lacan calls the Imaginary as their form of self-definition and of their development of an identification with blindness.

The three also imagine blindness in relation to sight. Their stories share the common goal of excluding negative identifications of and with blindness. While all their stories are similar to Frank's "restitution stories," they differ insofar as blindness does mark a sense of termination and finality as it is understood as an abnormal physical condition. Their similarity resides in the notion of sight and seeing as the standard for "normal life." Thus, their stories are not intended to remove blindness and to reconstitute their lives as sighted; instead, their stories are intended to reconstitute any negative identification with blindness into an image positively identified with an instrumental image of sight as skill and competence.

The mirror into which blindness looks reveals the ego ideal of skill and competence. What blindness in the Imaginary dreads seeing in its mirror image is the Real of blindness—the bewilderment of the initial chaos of not seeing in a world understood as something to be seen. "The restitution voice," says Frank (1994, 10), "speaks from the Imaginary, as the ill person is expected to recognize himself in images of health." Disabled people speak from, what might be called, the "adaptive narrative," and from this position of the Imaginary, disabled people are expected to recognize themselves in images of the "normal body" as skill and competence. Hence, expressions such as "differently abled." The difference of disability is imagined as a difference in ability, which requires an orientation to "ability"—different as it might be—conceived of as the ability to do the things that nondisabled people do "normally," such as move about the world, work, go to movies, or eat in restaurants. The adaptive story narrates the expectation that through adaptive procedures, including technology, disabled people develop the "different ability" to do the "normal things" of "normal life."

Adaptive narrative privileges this version of normalcy and deemphasizes disability as different in any other way from difference in ability. A version of this adaptive narrative was expressed by a participant at a disability symposium at which I recently spoke. A woman asked me about "blindisms." She said that it is necessary to remedy blindisms if blind people are to participate in the "sighted world," as she put it. Rehabilitation—another form of the adaptive narrative—has the same concern: "*Gently bring to your child's attention actions that detract from easy communication with the sighted.* There are actions required of the visually impaired child that are primarily responses to the sighted person's needs, and that have little purpose from a non-visual perspective. For example, turning to face the person being addressed, or who is addressing you, or being still when speaking" (Harrison and Crow 1993, 71; their italics). These authors go on to explain that, without visual stimulation, a blind child may develop bodily behaviors referred to by the authors as "mannerisms." "This lack of visual stimulus causes him to find substitute ways of meeting his needs. Usually, these are body oriented—rocking, bouncing, hand flapping, eye poking, masturbating, vocalizing, head banging, etc. Unless ways are found to prevent or curtail this socially unacceptable behaviour, it can become a habit" (238).

Not only are these behaviors socially unacceptable, according to the authors, they are also "caused" by blindness conceived of as "lack of visual stimuli." Felicity Harrison and Mary Crow call these behaviors "mannerisms" and the woman at the symposium referred to them as "blindisms." Either way, they are "isms" understood as inherent to those who are blind, particularly those who are congenitally so. The "ism" character of these behaviors are both recognized and find their cogency within the interpretive standard of blind people interacting in a "sighted world" and with sighted people. Not being inherent to sight, these behaviors are "seen" by sighted people as strange and interactionally disconcerting. Harrison and Crow, as well as the woman at the symposium, refigure these behaviors into the objective states of "mannerisms" and "blindisms." This reconfiguration "naturally" flows into the development of a rehabilitation program aimed at remedying these "isms" lest they become habitual.

This remedial practice is illustrative of the recommended movement from the Real of blindness into the Imaginary. Not looking toward the voice of the person with whom you are speaking, flapping your hands, poking your eyes are not voices of the adaptive narrative. These voices are strange and they cause sighted people to become bewildered. The voice of the Real of blindness is bewilderment and it is impossible to speak from this position in the voice of the "differently abled" in the midst of the "abled voices."

No wonder that Harrison and Crow and the woman at the symposium want to remove these blindisms before they become habitual. But what is being removed and with what are these blindisms being replaced? Sightisms? Is there such a thing? Or are blindisms not being replaced with any thing? Harrison and Crow (1993) lay out an entire rehabilitation program that demonstrates the methodic (and gentle) removal of blindisms. Not engaging in blindisms, they argue, is just as habitual as is engaging in them. Looking toward the voice of people with whom you are speaking is habit forming and so is not poking your eyes. Not acting blind can be habit forming and even though this cannot restore sight, it can show a commitment to adapting to blindness by adopting "sighted ways."

From the rehabilitation point of view, it becomes essential that blind people imagine what it is to see and, in this, to begin themselves to "see" that "blindisms" are bewildering and disturb interaction between blind and sighted people. The removal of "blindisms" requires that a blind person habituate himself or herself to imagining a world of visual stimuli. Blind people are encouraged to construct an identity through this image, but, as Frank (1994, 10) says, "Images, despite their inadequacy, are all the self has with which to construct an identity for itself. In these images the self must recognize itself or remain fragmented and formless." Imagining a life with visual stimuli when none exists provides for the inadequacy of any blind person's acting within and from the image of visual stimuli. Habituation is thus the only recourse for the development of a social identity. Without this "image of sight," blindisms depict both a blind person's fragmentation from interaction and the formlessness of his or her interaction bereft of any image of visual stimuli. The rehabilitative removal of "blindisms," then, amounts to the habituation of the construction of a blind person's social identity through the habitual imagining of what it means to see—specifically, of what it means to "see blindisms."

For blind people, forming the habit of recognizing one's self in the image of sight and what it means to see is, of course, done without sight. "The self that is constructed from these alter images is then haunted by a sense of lack that is not particular to any individual (though each person experiences his lack as distinctly his own) but endemic to being human. What the self lacks is, simply, itself: an unmediated vision of the self's coherence" (Frank 1994, 10). The particularity of the lack of sight that generates the need to habitually imitate sightedness derives its meaning from the adaptation narrative. Adapting to the image of the "sighted world" does not restore sight, it simply acts as demonstration; it demonstrates a blind person's commitment to participating in humanity as well as in a self understanding that she lacks. This is the quintessential adaptation narrative; it depicts the subject as understanding that he lacks and that he is committed to imitating the Other, but with a commitment that shows a recognition that he is only an image and not the Other. The truth in the cliché that imitation is the highest form of flattery is borne out in blind people's desire to participate in a world by depicting an image of the very thing they lack (sight) and by demonstrating their self-understanding of the need to overcome this lack.

This version of "disability identity" spoken in the voice of the adaptation narrative is most articulate in the fields of rehabilitation, special education, and other professional forms of mainstreaming. It is Lacan's Imaginary and Frank's restitution narrative. These narratives conceive of self-development and identity construction as a necessary stage in the life of an individual. Only an individual—not society, not the world—can be blind. It is, therefore, the individual who must adapt (be rehabilitated). The Imaginary understands blindness as a "sighted person with the sight missing." What is left for the blind person is to fill the void of this lack with the image of sight. The Imaginary sees nothing political here. It sees only the dichotomy of blindness and sightedness, of disability and nondisability. It sees the former as lack and the latter as a "reality" to which the former must adapt. Rehabilitation and other forms of mainstreaming learn nothing essential from disability since, for them, disability represents only lack. What they do learn stems from the gathering of information of "what works" for the process of "fitting" disabled people into the mainstream of society. The voice of mainstreaming is truly a monologue in the same way that Frank (1994,10) argues that medicine is a monologue in the conversation of illness as it takes place in the Imaginary. There is no exchange and the imitation engaged in by disabled people—in whatever form it takes—is the representation of "normalcy" as, to bring back Overboe (1999, 24), the "benchmark of humanity."

Bound to the Image

But what do we make of a "disability identity" bound to the image of "normalcy"? In the preceding chapters, I suggest that disability is more than lack; yet, in some sense, it is lack: lack of eyesight, lack of the ability to hear, lack of the ability to walk, and so on. Clearly, the environment is constructed—both literally and figuratively—on the basis of seeing, hearing, and walking and on the basis of many other "abilities." It is just as clear that the disability movement and subsequent legislation has not ended the fight for full accessibility and the environment remains significantly inaccessible to us. We (disabled people) imagine ourselves as participating and as participants in society and we ask for, and often demand, accommodations that would make the environment accessible to us.

This demand is based on an image of disability that goes beyond the individual. It brings the physical and social environment, cultural portrayals of the body, and collective representations of normalcy and abnormalcy together into a gestalt that collectively works to generate the phenomenon of disability. The three features that I heuristically call the environment, culture, and society are the parent(s) of disability and in their transmogrification give birth not to One but to a Manyness of disability. In the same way that Macnaughten and Urry 1995 suggests that there are "many natures," there are many disabilities. There are as many disabilities as there are transmogrifications of the environment, culture, and society. The difficulty with this formulation is that it subjugates disability to the refashioning of culture and society. Any image of disability is thus dependent on how culture and society conceive of themselves. The Manyness of disability is thus collapsed into the Oneness of dependence.

I conclude this book by developing a version of disability that seeks to liberate it from this subjugation and dependence. While disability may be metaphorically spoken of as a child of culture and society, this child has not become its parents. Still, children often reflect their parents and disability is no different; the question now is, What is the nature of this reflection? I turn now to an interrogation of the reflexive character of disability in society.

6

Image and Imitation

ontemporary society understands disability as lack and subsequently treats it as lack, particularly the lack of ability, figuring it within the frame of instrumental relations. The lack of the ability to see or to hear or to walk is framed within the inability to do things that ordinarily and naturally adhere to these abilities. This understanding leads to a conception of disability as essentially the "problem of inability."

And who can argue with this thinking? If you cannot walk, you certainly cannot climb a long and steep flight of stairs; if you cannot hear, you certainly cannot use the telephone; if you cannot see, you certainly cannot read a book. Or can you? This is the question (and the only question) that arises when disability is understood as the problem of inability. And who can argue with this question? Any argument would presuppose that far from being a problem of inability, disability is inability itself.

This is where the politics of disability comes in; this is where decisions are made. Are there ways to get around the problem of inability? Of course, this question is preceded by the question of worthwhileness: Is searching for ways to get around the problem of inability worth the trouble? Are there some disabilities that produce so much lack, so much inability, that futility gets in the way of even seeing a problem to be circumvented in the first place? As up-to-date as contemporary society is, these questions of worthwhileness are not always answered in the affirmative. But when they are, other decisions are made that implicitly achieve the relationship between disability and society.

Disability and Society

Whatever else disability is, it is a phenomenon that exists in the complex web of society, in the midst of social relations. How a society is organized shapes the appearance of disability. What counts as both a disability and its meaning are fashioned within the framework of societal organization. Different social patterns of this organization generate different accounts of disability, including different versions of appropriate societal responses to it. It is not my intention to develop a historical account of how disability took on its contemporary meaning.[1] Instead, I focus on contemporary understandings and subsequent treatments of disability and continue my overall project of trying to delineate the contemporary set of social relations that are disability.

One way to begin to explicate the connection between disability and contemporary society is to frame it, at least for the moment, within the paradigm of a "struggle." The struggle is not about whether or not disability should be included in society, for where else can it be? Rather, the struggle is over how disability should be included. Inclusion, however, has taken on a very specific meaning in contemporary understandings of disability; it is posed as the ultimate solution to the problem of exclusion. Disability is conceived of instrumentally insofar as it represents an "abnormalcy" in relation to the body understood in functional terms. The "natural body," as functional, comes equipped with the organic and mechanical predisposition to develop such functions as walking, hearing, seeing, and the rest. The "disabled body" is posited as lacking one or more of these functions. Both disability and nondisability can thus be framed within this instrumental conception of the body.

This body-of-functions now finds itself instrumentally placed in the environment, both the physical and social ones. The body's inclusion in the environment turns on this conception. The body can now sense the environment; it can see it, hear it, smell it; it can move through the environment, walk and run through it; it can manipulate the environment and intellectually conceive of things and build them with hands and arms; it can reproduce itself by eating and drinking that which is provided by the environment and find shelter in it. The same holds true for the built or social environment. The body, with its body-of-functions intact, can perceive and move through the social institutions of kinship, education, and leisure, as well as participate in the rest of the social, political, and economic institutions of society. The body-of-function provides for the possibility of the inclusion of individuals into the environment—the one that is natural and the one that is made.

This formulation of the connection between the body and the environment is what Judith Shklar (1990, 5) refers to as the "given." Both people and the environment are treated as given, as "natural" but also as distinct from each other. A version of inclusion that rests on a given—or rule of nature—will also have an equally natural version of exclusion. A "natural body" leads naturally to inclusion while an "unnatural body" leads just as naturally to exclusion. This formulation does not recognize anything decisive about itself. There is nothing political or even social about this formulation. Bodies either function or do not and, on this basis, people either are included or are excluded. The decisive (political) character of this instrumental relation to inclusion and exclusion becomes lost in its own instrumentality.

This instrumentality remains the basis for the dominant conception of disability in contemporary society. There is no argument from this side that disabled people are excluded from full participation in society; exclusion is understood as a natural function of disability. We (disabled people) cannot do some of the things nondisabled people can do and, therefore, we are excluded from some of the things that nondisabled people participate in. This is all quite "natural" and moreover it presents disability as a "natural problem." The "problem of disability" becomes the problem of inability. Exclusion is taken as a given and the problem of inability becomes the problem of inclusion. How are disabled people to do things? How can they be included? These are the orienting questions of the contemporary engagement with disability.

What's the Difference?

Disability understood as the problem of inability is the implicit answer to the question, What's the difference? The answer is that disabled people *are different*, but only in the way we do things. We are unable to do things in the way that nondisabled people do. Still, we (can) do these things but we do them differently; hence, the contemporary usage "differently abled." Inability and ability become collapsed under this rubric of difference.

The inclusion or integration of disabled people thus turns on the inclusion of this difference; disability, and any social identity that springs from it, is brought under the umbrella of this difference in ability. An identification with disability as well as a disability identity is woven with the threads of the doing of things, albeit doing them differently. The following appears in a Canadian Government report on disability entitled *In Unison* (Federal, Provincial, and Territorial Ministers 1998, 8): "Persons with disabilities participate as full citizens in all aspects of Canadian society. The full participation of persons with disabilities requires the commitment of all segments of society. The realization of the vision will allow persons with disabilities to maximize their independence and enhance their well-being through access to required supports and the elimination of barriers that prevent their full participation." This report says that its "key organizing concept" is "inclusion"—the "full inclusion" of persons with disabilities in Canadian society (16). What is puzzling about this report's "vision" is that it "sees" disabled people as participating and not participating at the same time. While we participate in all aspects of Canadian society (and do so as full citizens), we (disabled people) require the commitment of all segments of society in order to do so, supports that will maximize our independence and well-being, and access to all segments of society as well as the elimination of barriers to such access. Even though we participate in society, *In Unison* documents a number of signs (especially high unemployment rates among disabled people [35–37]) of our lack of participation. The "vision" of full participation is yet to be realized, according to the report. Yet, it suggests that disabled people are included and do participate in all aspects of Canadian society.

The key to this seeming contradiction is that while disabled people do participate as full citizens, we do not participate (real or imagined) *in the way* nondisabled people do. Thus, what is at issue is the way disabled people participate and are included in society and not participation and inclusion per se.

> To initiate an analysis of the social workings of disability by way of its integration is a method more critical, even more militant, than to address it in terms of exclusion. The motives and factors that lead to rejection, even when such rejection is hidden and subtle, are fairly obvious to the attentive. Integration passes more unnoticed. Sometimes it even seems to occur on its own. It embodies claims that are widely supported today. Everything contributes to masking the reasons for integration, to forgetting them, to jumbling the various means of integration under the aegis of an ethics of integration. From the moment you integrate, who would venture to come looking for how it happens, why it happens, and in the way it does? (Stiker 1999, 15–16)

If Henri-Jacques Stiker's idea of "integration" is taken as an alternative usage for inclusion and participation, what does such an idea tell us about the "social workings of disability"? The exclusion of disabled people is obvious even to the bureaucratic attentiveness of government officials and *In Unison* documents this exclusion quite clearly and quite dramatically. But what of participation? Other than claiming that disabled people participate as full citizens in all aspects of Canadian society, *In Unison* says nothing more about this participation. In fact, it goes immediately on to document exclusion, the need for inclusion, and a strategy for achieving it. The participation of disabled people in Canadian society is a "vision," according to *In Unison*, yet to be realized. The participation of disabled people that *In Unison* notices is quite technical and quite obvious—we are citizens. Participation is our right—a right both recognized and granted to us. But, as Jerome Bickenbach (1993, 163) points out, we (disabled people) cannot exercise our right to participate in all aspects of society if these "aspects" are not accessible to us. Disabled people are thus "full citizens" without being an essential part of the citizenry.

The problem—how to integrate citizens into the citizenry. The solution—treat all citizens as participants in the citizenry with the stipulation that some citizens participate differently from others. The "vision" of *In Unison* amounts to what Stiker calls an "ethics of integration." What such an ethos masks and jumbles is another question. Any ethics of integration or inclusion includes some understanding of the "difference" that requires inclusion. It requires also a version of this "difference" that makes inclusion possible within the parameters of normative inclusion. Disability must be seen as something that can be included into the existing social structure of society without essentially changing that structure. Any modification (accommodation) that is designed to make an environment accessible to disabled people must be "reasonable"—it should not cost too much, nor should it change the environment too much. The difference should be minimal.

In Unison implicitly recommends a version of the difference that can be employed in order to provide for the possibility of disability's inclusion in society. The report speaks of disabled people in person-first language—"persons with disabilities." This language achieves two things: first, it dichotomizes "person" and "disability" by positing the latter as a condition, disability is with a person. Then, this language privileges personhood and deemphasizes disability by invoking it as an unessential feature of (with) a person (Titchkosky 2001). The overall effect of such language use is to minimize the difference-of-disability in favor of the sameness-of-personhood. Disabled people's "citizenship" thus resides in the social fact of our status as persons and not in our conditional status as "disabled." While our disabilities may make it difficult, and sometimes even impossible, to participate in the citizenry, our personhood grants us citizenship . . . like everyone else.

The Removal of Difference

The linguistic and thus interactional removal of difference as a method for the achievement of sameness is certainly not something restricted to bureaucratic orientations to life such as are found in *In Unison*. This is precisely the method I employed when I passed as a fully sighted person. All of my linguistic and interactional "moves" were oriented to achieving my self as a "normally seeing" person. My standard was a "normal person" with all the rights, privileges, and obligations that came with it. The "rights and obligations" that I had in mind, though, were the things that sighted people had both a right and an obligation to see. The "privilege" was the privilege of "normalcy" that I could acquire through the interactional achievement of such rights and obligations. My goal in passing was to demonstrate that I was worthy of the privilege that came from being "normal" and I demonstrated my worthiness by "seeing" the things I had a right to "see" together with the things I was obliged to "see."[2]

Although my passing during adolescence was designed to hide my legal blindness, I continued to pass when such "hiding" was no longer my goal. I did, and continue to do, what many blind people do: I look toward the voice of the person with whom I am speaking; I conduct myself in public with the "knowledge" that I am visually available to others, and so I dress appropriately, I do not scratch certain parts of my body; I use phrases such as "See you later," "I watched TV," "I saw that movie," and so on. I face the students while I teach my classes and move around and use all sorts of body gestures as I lecture and I accept and grade term papers—actual printed words on paper. I do all of these things; I show others as well as myself that I can do them. I can get to my classroom "like everyone else," albeit differently since my guide dog Smokie guides me there. I can sense and know my environment, although I do it differently, without sight. Most important to the standard of normalcy, I can demonstrate that I know that standard and can act in it "standardly," although I do it differently. In ways such as these, I can show that, like everyone else, I am not everyone else, but I sure am "like them." Like everyone else, I too can participate "like everyone else," even if I have to do it differently. It is important—to everyone else—that I do things like everyone else no matter how differently I do them, so long as I do them—like everyone else.

As a child, and even, though to a lesser degree, as an adolescent, I had a sense of my disability but less in the sense of an "abnormality" and more in the sense of "ill health." The "something wrong with my eyes" had more to do with illness insofar as my eyes lost their healthy character. My eyes were no longer healthy and were no longer like the healthy eyes of others; my eyes were unhealthy. After all, my parents had taken me to an eye doctor and later I went to several more on my own. All of these doctors gave me a diagnosis, even though there was some disagreement among them. Where there is no disagreement is in the prognosis—there is no cure for my condition and my eyesight will steadily deteriorate as I grow older.

Doctors, tests, diagnosis, prognosis—all of these practices fell under the rubric of what even as a child I understood as medicine. This medicalization of my eyesight framed my experience as illness and dominated my experience till adolescence, when it began to lose its cogency. There was no cure and my unhealthy eyes were going to stay that way; there was no pain, no hospitalization, not even a need for bed rest and, most important, there was no "mark" of ill health—no deformity, no eye patches, nothing. I was not so very different from anyone else—at least in appearance—even though what "appeared" to me was very different. This standard of appearance and image began to dominate my sense of myself during adolescence. I could, and did, achieve an image of my self as "normal" and I focused my life on the construction of just such an appearance. I took myself out of the realm of stigmatization, pity, charity case and in doing so removed myself from the realm of illness.

The change I made is reminiscent of what Stiker (1999, 140) describes on a macro level in his historical study of disability in Europe, particularly in France: "The disabled have been lost in the mass of the indigent; now they are recognized, shown consideration, and put to one side in order to be made 'like everyone else'!" In an effort to appear "like everyone else," I put my disability (difference) to one side. Putting it aside is, in fact, the fundamental interactional method for removing any cogency that difference has. This spatial and geographic metaphor—putting to one side—is particularly salient for understanding the "place of disability" in contemporary society.

> Every impaired person becomes . . . someone who lacks a place and not just an organ or a faculty, someone for whom a place has to be made. Not a place offering sociability or a place of social networks but simply in society, in the

social fact . . . for good or ill, the disabled were exceptions and stood for exceptionality, alterity; now that they have become ordinary, they have to be returned to ordinary life, to ordinary work. . . . rehabilitation marks the appearance of a culture that attempts to complete the act of identification, of making identical. This act will cause the disabled to disappear and with them all that is lacking, in order to assimilate them, drown them, dissolve them in the greater and single social whole. (Stiker 1999, 128)

My act of setting aside my blindness to concentrate on appearance and image illustrates Stiker's notion of the "place of disability" in society. I set aside exceptionality in favor of a return to ordinary life. Such a change represents a movement of realms. The medicalization of disability places it into the realm of illness, with its grammar of cure, providing for the possibility of understanding disability as temporary. This I did for a while; before I put my disability aside, I put it "up front" and set about "ophthalmology hopping," looking for a cure. Placing disability in the realm of illness leads to a "faith in medicine" mentality that is exploited on a societal level in efforts to raise funds for medical research. These efforts often tastelessly invoke sympathy to elicit donations. Faith in medicine is often commingled with a faith in the strength of the human spirit: I *will* see again, or, in Christopher Reeve's case, I *will* walk again.

Sooner or later, however, society (even medicine) comes to see that there are many disabilities that are incurable. Many individuals come to the same conclusion and the problem of disability now becomes the problem of place, both individually and collectively. If disabled people are not ill or indigent, what are they? If disabled people are "just" disabled, where do they belong? Or, better, where should they be moved? Disability is no longer a temporary feature of society (of the social fact), but a permanent one. Disability becomes as social and factual as the social fact of society itself. As social fact, we (disabled people) lose our exceptionality, as Stiker says. Our place is in the scenography of the ordinary found in the ordinariness of the social fact of society. Even though society is the place of disability, it (society) is reluctant to give disability a place. What will society do with all of us who lack organs and faculties? After all, society "built itself" only for those who have organs and faculties. Society intended itself only for those whose "ordinariness" is fashioned within the imaginary of nondisability. Making a place for disability is out of the question; too much time, money, and energy have been placed into fashioning the artifice of society; everything is already organized. There is a panoply of stairs, printed material, and parks and playgrounds to run and play in, and there are ordinary ways to "look" and be "seen" as ordinary. It is just unreasonable to make a place for disability. But maybe, just maybe, disability can be made to fit into the already existing place of society. Perhaps, if disability could rid itself of its exceptionality and its difference, perhaps then, it can become ordinary enough to "fit into" ordinary society.

Enter rehabilitation: its overall goal, according to the *Oxford English Dictionary*, is to restore disability to a previous condition where such a condition is conceived of as the imagined "original human condition" of ordinariness—difference aside, we are all people, we are all like everyone else, we all put our pants on one leg at a time, at least we should imagine ourselves as doing so. We all know that we are all visually available to one another, even if some of us cannot "ordinarily see" one another. Still, if we get rid of our "blindisms" (recall Harrison and Crowe and the woman at the disability symposium), we can appear as if we "ordinarily see" everyone else, just like everyone else does. Perhaps we can be rehabilitated, or rehabilitate ourselves, and restore our ordinary human right to be "ordinarily human."

This is the quintessential version of the "adaptive narrative" regarding disability. The standard for disabled people is not actually nondisability and normalcy but ordinariness. It is the ordinariness that derives from the reduction of everyone (all difference) to the nebulous interpretive category—people. We are all identical insofar as we can all identify with this category. Literally anything that can be interpreted as exceptionality, difference, good, bad, anything can be erased through the invocation of this "people." Despite our exceptionality or difference, we are at bottom people, ordinary people. Extraordinariness, of whatever kind, is accounted for by conceiving of it as a feature of ordinariness. Without ordinariness, nothing extraordinary can occur and, as a corollary, anything extraordinary can be erased. And after all the erasing is done, what remains is the essential and indelible mark of ordinariness—people.

Disabled people, like everyone else, bear the mark of ordinariness. Forms of exclusion and discrimination arise from a certain understanding of disability: when the difference of the "extraordinary body" (Thomson 1996, 1997a) is conceived of as "freakery" or as "defect" or as "abnormalcy," and when this is transposed as the essential identity of anyone who is disabled, exclusion and discrimination are always-already an aspect of such transposition. This is the auspices under which contemporary society seeks to include and integrate disabled people. If disabled people are to be included in society, their disability must be viewed as something other than an essentializing feature of their identity. Hence, the contemporary trope toward deemphasizing disability and privileging personhood. As extra-ordinary and as defective and abnormal as disabled people are, they are still essentially people and thus essentially ordinary. The standard for measuring the inclusion of disabled people in society, therefore, becomes the same as the one for nondisabled people, ordinariness. The battle for inclusion of disabled people becomes the battle for ordinariness, a sense of "seeing past a disability" to the ordinary person. This "battle" is forged against the "enemy" of the impulse and temptation to "see" (interpret) disabled people strictly on the basis of their extraordinariness. Seeing and treating nondisabled people as ordinary is never a battle, because they embody sameness and they are identical insofar as they are "like everyone else." The same is not true for those of us who are disabled. There is a continuous need to "look past our disabilities" and to "look for our ordinariness." This "looking," like any other form of looking, sometimes results in "seeing" and sometimes not. The upshot is that the contemporary requirement of needing to erase disability will, ironically, result in the continuation of exclusionary practices toward disability.

> I am not saying that exclusion will disappear. I am saying that the problem of our society is not a failure to integrate but of integrating too well, integrating in such a way that identicalness reigns, at least a rough identity, a socially constructed identity, an identity of which citizens can be convinced. That is to say, when we know the strength of a consensus, there is an identity no less real than if it had actually been achieved, for social imaginings are just as effectively social as the material or objective situation of things and people. (Stiker 1999, 132)

Stiker is not suggesting that our society has integrated disabled people so well that exclusion has been erased and will never again appear on the face of society. Instead, I read him as speaking of a "consensus of ordinariness," as speaking of an imagined social identity constructed upon (and constructing) the imagined "identicalness" of the standard of ordinariness for all—all citizens are ordinary citizens. It is only on the basis of this standard of ordinariness that our society seeks to include disabled people. As Stiker says, "Disabled people are admitted, readmitted as we say, if—and only if—the disability is no more than a secondary feature of the same order as height, hair color, or weight. The disabled person is integrated only when the disability is erased" (151–52).

The trope to identify the difference of disability with that of height, hair color, and weight is a turn "to rejoin the group of the able" (Stiker 1999, 143). Rejoining this group means, foremost, that disability must be both seen and treated as a form of unessential and ordinary difference allowing for "the fall into reintegration among the crowd of normals" (143). Hence—"I am five feet nine inches tall and weigh one hundred and seventy pounds. My eyes are blue; oh, and by the way, those blue eyes?—they don't see." As ordinary and as "by the way" as our society would have blindness, it remains an imagined ordinariness and a social construction of blindness as ordinary. Society remains an artifice constructed by and for people who see. It is not that blind people and sighted people are the same; that you ordinarily "see" the world while I ordinarily do not, does not make us the same; for one thing, I see a different world from what you see and, for another, I do not have the same access to the world that you have. Even though, as Stiker (1999, 150) says, "The face of society should not have any pimples," blindness is not merely an ordinary adolescent case of acne. "Clearing up" blindness requires something more than outgrowing it. It is in the Lacanian sense of the Imaginary where some abstract version of able-bodiedness creates disability as the same as a case of acne. But, "Would that we could all be the same!" (150). Society's wish, as expressed through its treatment of disability, is to make identical, without making equal.

As ordinary and thus as identical as we (disabled people) are, we are certainly not equal. As willing as society is to bring persons in, it is not always as willing for persons to bring their disabilities in with them. Inclusion on the basis of privileging personhood over disability is thus never inclusionary. The difference-of-disability is always excluded in this version of inclusion. Social change is never part of such an inclusion. "But disability cannot be a confrontational position, a force for social change, a mutant or a revolutionary minority. In other words, the disabled should always adapt to society such as it is" (Stiker 1999, 137).

But what is the nature of this "adaptation" and of this society, "such as it is"? Using the work of Stiker, I have attempted to show how ordinariness acts as the imagined standard for the interpretation and treatment of disabled people in contemporary society. I have also tried to show how this standard mediates the difference between disability and nondisability to make the two the same while preserving the dichotomy between them. To fully understand Stiker's insights on the relationship between disability and society, however, they must be developed. Some version of contemporary society, with its disabled and nondisabled citizens, which Stiker does not specify, must be at work in this act of "saming." I return now to something I raise earlier in this chapter as a way to develop Stiker's insights.

The Doing of Things and the Problem of Inability

Stiker (1999) shows how industrialization influences society's ideological understanding of humanness. One of the ideas that industrialization brings along is the sense of the "normal individual." This norming (Davis 1995), together with the ideologies of production and progress, strengthens and reifies the notion of people as "able" and as possessing "abilities." Industrialization generates the new idea of a work force along with the understanding that "normal" and thus ordinary people are now eligible and even obliged to participate in the overall relations of societal production. This understanding is the basis for Paul Abberley's suggestion (1988, 92) that disability should be treated as a "human being" rather than a "human doing" and it is also the basis for Thomson's concept of "normate culture" (1997a).

Participation in society now includes a strong sense of the ability to do things. The Industrial Revolution calls forth an individual who is judged primarily on his or her ability to do things in terms of "making a living" as well as in terms of "contributing" to the economy. These things are then seen as the sort of things that any normal and ordinary person would do and would desire to do. The ordinary ability to make a living and to contribute to the economy becomes tied to the necessary version of the individual as one who possesses a body conceived of as a body-of-functions.

Bodies (individuals) are now interpreted and judged on the basis of this ordinary body-of-functions that are inexorably tied to the good of making a living and contributing to society. Industrialization refigures participation in society as contribution to it. Those interpreted as not possessing the ordinary body-of-functions are judged unable to make a living and thus unable to contribute to society. What stands between the "inability" to participate in and contribute to society is the possession of this ordinary body-of-functions—the "ability" to do things. The problem of disability thus becomes the problem-of-inability.

Making disabled people identical with nondisabled ones requires this problem insofar as any problem of inability, especially in modern times, coexists with the idea of solution. Industrialization, with its sense of hypertechnology, presents techné as the fundamental solution to any problem. "America [and Canada] seems to be a nation built on the premise that, with great effort and the right technique, there is no mountain that cannot be climbed and no force of nature that cannot go unharnessed. . . . Faith in the technological cure encourages belief in the fallacy that all problems have a technical solution" (Zola 1988, 370). Whatever the problem might be, technology can be invented to solve it. This is the grounds for contemporary society's version of disability as a technical problem. The modern version of techné conjoins the doing of things with the problem of such doing, making them identical. Disability and ability commingle in their identical commitment to the doing of things, and in this commitment, both disabled people and nondisabled people are ordinary and, as such, are the same.

This sentiment was expressed in an interview I conducted with Susan (2000), director of a Disability Resource Centre at a large university.

Susan: The other thing is the students tend to, ah, use the resource
room a lot, because they need the equipment. So, they get to
meet each other and as they meet each other, and see what
equipment they're using, they start problem-solving together too
and exchanging ideas. Ah, and now for example they have the
young adult group. So, its even more formalized and maybe . . .
Interviewer: So, this is a support group for students with disabilities?
Susan: Yeah, with visual impairments, yeah. So they know each other
even better and help each other.

Visually impaired students come together in the resource room because of need; they need the equipment. Susan is speaking here of assistive computer technology. As these students come together, they get
to know each other and begin to "problem solve" together. This infor-
mal problem-solving is even more formalized in the "young adult
group." The "ideas" that the students share and the "help" and "support" they give one another are, according to Susan, based solely on
technology.

What brings these disabled students together is their need for technology. What keeps them together, both informally and formally, is
their need to share ideas and information about technology. Without
technology, these visually impaired students would not be able to do
the ordinary things of university life; they would not be able to read
books, write papers, take notes in class, and so on. They "come together" under the auspices of an identity set in the frame of the problem-of-inability and this identity is understood as their need. According to Susan's account, their identification with disability as the
problem-of-inability collects them and provides them with the understanding that technology is the quintessential solution to the problem
of disability. That their disability can be solved technically makes
them the *same* as any other student because any other (nondisabled)
student also does the ordinary things of university life technically.
Nondisabled students may come together to discuss techniques for
writing term papers, studying for exams, getting a good grade from a
certain professor, and so on. Visually impaired students come together
to discuss techniques for reading books, writing term papers, and taking notes in class. This is the ordinary "doing of university things" of

any "ordinary" student; it is all a matter of technique; it is as technically simple as that.

Susan does not notice whether the visually impaired students are discussing anything other than technique and technology. Her "noticing" is informed by the context of Disability Resource Centre as an essentially technical one. The problem-of-inability generates a "need" for resources understood as technical. University life is framed for disabled students not only by the notion of the doing of things but also by the doing of certain things—the technical things of university student life such as the techniques of reading and writing. There is nothing political or even social about this for Susan, it is strictly a technical matter. Visually impaired students cannot do the ordinary things of university life and technology permits them to do these things.

Thus, these students' identities are bound up with a notion of inability and a subsequent need to remedy it. "Disability identity" becomes concretized as a technical problem in need of a technical solution. Susan's interpretation of the "problem-solving" in which the students are engaged is restricted to a search for a solution to the problem of inability. Identity as disabled is not a problem in need of a solution since it has already been solved; a "disability identity" has already been solved insofar as it is identified with, and identical to, a "nondisability identity." Both identities are wrapped in the materiality of the "doing of things," which acts to essentialize the "human identity." The "coming together" of these visually impaired students is collected under the auspices of such an identification. When the students "come together," they are depicting their togetherness as identical to this human identity, as identical to the "doers of things." The "coming together" of visually impaired students in the resource room represents the coming together of disability and nondisability. Any difference between the two is understood as the unessential difference that comes from doing things differently. The only difference disability makes is collected (comes together) under the sameness of techné; everyone does things and everyone makes use of techniques and technologies to do them. The difference-of-disability can now be erased with the invocation of the contemporary rhetoric that seeks to persuade both disabled and nondisabled people that doing things differently is a difference that does not make a difference. The idea of techné as the "universal equalizer" and thus as the quintessential solution to the problem of disability is evoked as the ultimate grounds for the inclusion of disabled people into society. This rationale is not only presented as the grounds for inclusion; it simultaneously depoliticizes and even desocializes both the desire for and practice of such inclusion.

That disabled students come together in a classroom with nondisabled others has no social or political significance for the socially organized practices of Disability Resource Centres. Susan continues in our interview to depict a difference between visually impaired students and learning disabled students.

So, so they [visually impaired students] know each other even better and help each other, while students with learning disabilities often cannot identify themselves in the classroom! So you could be sitting next to a student with a learning disability—you have a learning disability—but you may have no way of knowing, yeah, unless you're using, for example, a notetaker or you're using extended time for tests and exams outside the classroom. All of a sudden students will click that they're both going down to the test room to do the test. But usually visually impaired students, ah, might be better able to recognize each other, ah, particularly if they use cane mobility. But, no, I mean you could be sitting next to a student in a classroom who is also, has quite a significant visual loss and not be aware of it if they, ah, have really good, ah, mobility, with that mobility you might not notice it.

For Susan, disabled students "knowing each other" equals "helping each other" and "helping" equals helping each other by sharing information about techniques and technologies for doing the things of university life such as taking notes in the classroom and writing exams. Knowing (identifying with) one another is mediated by technology. In fact, the signifier of disability is technology. Learning-disabled students do not recognize one another except through the use of techniques such as a "notetaker" or "extended time" for writing tests and exams. Except for the "young adult group," visually impaired students are in the same boat. They identify with each other through mobility techniques such as "cane mobility." These signifiers "mark" their difference from nondisabled students, and their identification with such difference is couched in technical terms. "Once they know each other," continues Susan, "they say, 'Hey, I write my exams this way' or 'I take notes that way' and then they start exchanging all kinds of techniques."

There is nothing peculiar about this sort of exchange, for university students, disabled or not, often exchange techniques for writing exams, taking notes in class, writing term papers, and so on. There is also nothing peculiar about a director of a university Disability Resource Centre focusing on the good of such an exchange given that her job is to provide technical resources for disabled university students. What is peculiar is that such a focus acts to occlude anything political about disability. It is peculiar that the only "exchange" that disabled students have—once they identify with one another—is animated and mediated by techné.

The source of this peculiarity resides elsewhere, however, than in the socially organized practices of university Disability Resource Centres, which are governed by the understanding that disability is solely a "technical problem" requiring techniques and technologies conceived of as the best solution to this "problem." This conception generates exchanges of techné as the most, if not the only, worthwhile exchange among disabled students. Identification with one another becomes focused on the requirement and worthwhileness of such an exchange. These students' "identification with disability" is enmeshed in the impoverished sense of the social understood as the exchange of technical information. This version of the social collects disabled students (brings them together) under the auspices of disability conceived of as the unessential difference of doing things differently.

The doing of things is certainly crucial for both disabled and nondisabled students and the techniques for doing them are equally important. Still, it is possible to imagine a conception of disability that can commingle with and even focus the technical understanding of disability. Such a conception would necessarily have to be more political than the technical one. It would threaten the implicit commitment to erasing any essential difference of disability held by the technical conception. It would result in a different sort of "coming together" as well as a different identification with disability and a different sense of a disability identity. To take a different example; imagine two women finding themselves in a classroom at medical school in a university in the 1950s. They would probably be the only women in that classroom. They might exchange information about the techniques of taking notes or writing exams. But they might also identify with each other as women. They would identify themselves as a minority—likely an unwelcome one—in the midst of a classroom and a profession dominated by men. Their "problem" would not be animated by techné; instead, it would be animated by the politics of difference located in minority group status. The exchange that springs from such an identification is far different and goes far beyond the exchanging of mere technical information. Doing the things of medical school and the prevention of such doings is rooted not in techné but in the discriminatory version of inclusion that stems from being part of a minority. The exchange that these women would have might focus on the political problem of minority inclusion and might even extend to an exchange of ideas regarding the difference that women make in the midst of the hegemony of a male-dominated society with its male-dominated professions. Their inclusion in medical school represents a very different "coming together" than does Susan's account of disabled students' inclusion in university. Womanness is a much more political identity in our not-so-fictitious example than is the disability identity found in our equally as real university Disability Resource Centre example.

Unlike other minority groups, disabled people are still viewed as people with a "condition." Their disability is seen as something that is theirs in-so-far as it is something that happened to them. This more privatized version of disability has social policy implications that turn on such a privatization. While governments recognize their role in legislation and policy development regarding disability, there remains an overriding sense of disability as an individual matter requiring individual adaptation. For example, I recently attended a government conference on disability issues. Despite current legislation and policy as it relates to society's role in resolving disability issues, the conference was entitled "Attitude Is Everything." "Attitude" referred to the attitude

of individual disabled persons. The conference included several pre-
sentations given by disabled people. One after another, these disabled
people told their story of how a "positive attitude" enabled them to
"overcome" their disability.

Susan expressed the same individualized and privatized version of
disability. She spoke of how government funding was available to
these students up to and including high school but was not available
when they entered university. "I also feel a certain amount of, ah, . . .
I don't know what the right word is . . . I, I would wish that more students with learning disabilities or their families challenge the government . . . and to say this is discrimination. You know, if every other
province recognizes learning disabilities, ah, if this province recognizes
them at the, ah, elementary and secondary level, then you're discrimi-
nating if all of a sudden at the college level you say you don't recognize
them." While Susan conceives of this discrepancy in funding as discrimination and thus as a social problem, she does not see the solution
in the same way. She does see the need to "challenge" this discrimination, but she "wishes" that this challenge would be mounted by
learning-disabled students or their families. The solution to the problem of even societal discrimination is located in the individual and
within the private realm of the family. Susan does not imagine any role
that the Disability Resource Centre can play in mounting such a challenge, but not because she is socially and politically irresponsible. On
the contrary, the unpolitical character of the Disability Resource Centre has very little to do with Susan herself. It has more to do with the
dominant societal conception of disability as an individual and private
matter. Susan is merely one tiny cog in this giant wheel. Even though
she is not personally responsible for such a conception and its subsequent depoliticization of disability, she is making implicit use of it
and is thus promoting disability as an individual and private matter.
Disability Resource Centres typically "center" their conception of
resources on the ideology of adaptation. These centers see their responsibility as "service providers"—as providers of adaptive technology to disabled students. They understand the "equitable distribution" of such technology as being outside the realm of their mandate.

The provision of existing technology to disabled students is one thing, challenging the inequitable and discriminatory character of such provision is another.

Even though contemporary society tends to view disability as an individual issue, there is something a little odd about this. There is no doubt that individual adaptation is a salient feature of current thinking about disability. It is equally true that this thinking has been extended, at least to some degree, to include society as well. Disabled individuals must adapt to the social environment and this environment must adapt to them by adding or including such features as curb cuts for wheelchairs and Braille markings on elevator pads. The idea and possibility of inclusion precedes both sets of adaptation. An individual must think that he or she is in an environment to which he or she belongs in order to adapt to it. Similarly, society must think that disability is in it and belongs in it in order for it to adapt to disability. However, to repeat, how disabled people are to be included in society is another question.

Whatever the form of inclusion, disabled individuals adapt and so does society. Adaptation, as it relates to disability, always includes a particular version of adjustment. Disabled persons adjust their selves in order to adapt; they makes adjustments to their bodies, to their expectations, to their aspirations. Finding herself in a wheelchair in her mid twenties, for example, a woman may adjust her aspiration of playing on the Canadian Olympic Ice Hockey Team, she may adjust her expectation of being "able" to enter any building, she will certainly have to adjust her body as she pushes, squeezes, and manipulates her body through her environment. She adjusts to the "fact" that her body is different from most others, and she adapts. The situation is somewhat different for society; it changes itself (slightly) and makes a few accommodations for disabled people and it even adapts its human rights legislation to include disabled people. But has it adjusted to disability? What adjustment has society made in order to adapt itself to disability? It certainly has not adjusted to the "social fact" of the presence of disability in its midst despite the omnipresence of disability from the very beginning of society. What society has adjusted to is the omnipresence of "misfortune," and its subsequent adaptation turns on the view that the "misfortune of disability" happens to only a few individuals. Society then adapts itself to these individuals by "doing what it can" to "help out" and since disability happens to only a few individuals, it remains an individual issue and not a societal one. Disabled people's membership in society is not the issue for societal adaptation to disability, cost is (Zola 1982, 244). It simply costs too much for society to adapt to disability, and so it will "do what it can."

Despite this omnipresent individualistic interpretation of disability, society will only "do what it can" if disabled people are the same as nondisabled ones. This sameness is based, as I have tried to show, on the idea that the doing of things is what brings (collects) disabled and nondisabled people together. Still, this "bringing-together" is not trouble free; it still engenders discomfort, fear, and pity and it still reminds nondisabled others as well as society of their fragility. As individualistic a matter as society likes to think disability is, it (society) still responds to it as representation. It is what disability represents that society is uncomfortable with and fears and it is this to which it responds. People-first language may thus be understood as one such response to this fear and discomfort. Try as it might, however, society has not quite been able to complete the individualization and privatization of disability and it continues to "battle" the nonindividualistic representation that is disability.

Stiker (1997, 60), in his discussion of disability and the ancient world, says of the disabled god Hephaestus:

His inherent weakness opens for him the domain of mysterious efficacy. The disability excludes him from a public role, from the structure of power (let us not forget the failure of Oedipus). But disability is in collusion with the whole underside of appearances and of the established; it allows his participation in another, secret face of things. Disability is not admitted to everyday organization; it is not *integrated* in that sense. But it opens the door to the arcane. The deformed being could play only an exceptional and not a current role, but he does play a role. The disabled god is left to his alterity; usually it is destabilizing and terrifying, but he has been given a function that is indicative, disruptive, subversive, prestigious, and theurgical. His fate is not in the least trivialized and, as an individual, he suffers most atrociously at times, but his alterity tears a certain veil that masks our ordinary arrangements. In the final analysis, the disabled person is never considered an *individual* who ought to be able to live among others; he is always considered a sign, a collective one "good to think about," as [Claude] Lévi-Strauss would say, "good to worry about," I would add.

What can we learn from this? Certainly not that disabled people are gods in contemporary society. Or, are we? No, there is nothing godlike about disability. Or, is there? We certainly evoke thoughts of God at times. There are times when nondisabled people "see us" and take this opportunity to "thank" God that they are not like us. A disabled woman at a conference I attended, speaking to a large audience, said that her disability was a "gift from God" and a "sign" that she now had a "special ability" to take on various social justice causes. If not gods, we are at least still surrounded by the arcane shroud of mystery.

Like Hephaestus, disabled people are still excluded from the public role and from societal structures of power. Disability is still in collusion with the underside of appearances and with the established. Even though we (disabled people) are not generally admitted to everyday organization, we still seek admittance, asking and fighting for accessibility to such organization. We still keep secret the "face of things" that our disabilities reveal to us. Our disabilities permit us the occasion to glimpse the "underside of appearances" as well as the assumptions that ground the established. At times, we grasp this secret face of things as a way to theorize the assumptions and values that lie under the appearances of our culture and society. At other times, we keep this secret face of things secret and, at still other times, these things remain secret even to us.

Not being admitted to everyday organization, we, like Hephaestus, are not integrated. We, too, can play only exceptional and not current roles. Even though contemporary society tries its utmost to "see" disability as ordinary, and even though disabled people and nondisabled ones alike try very hard to see the same thing—to see disabled people as "just like anyone else"—this "ordinary role" is itself seen as exceptional. The current version of exceptionality in relation to disability is that disabled people are ordinary and are "just like everyone else"; this is exceptional. It is both exceptional and difficult to see; seeing the ordinary in the extraordinary is as difficult as seeing the extraordinary in the ordinary. The door to the arcane buried deeply in the ordinary is what is open to disability. Contemporary society, however, formulates the problem of disability the other way around. It steers disability only in the direction of the ordinary. The door that opens onto the extraordinary character of the ordinary is avoided. The only mystery to and of disability that resonates in contemporary society is how disabled people, ordinary as we are, are to open the tightly shut and bolted door of the ordinary.

As terrifying as disability is to any version of the ordinary, it does have its function and its possibilities. Beyond its theurgical function, disability is "indicative" of the fragility of the human body and is "subversive" in its power to indicate the fragility of the body politic as well. Yet, disability possesses the inherent "prestige" of the possibility to disrupt. The disruption of contemporary hegemonic ideas of reason over passion and of mind over body is perhaps disability's greatest possibility. Disability disrupts society's carefully structured and multilayered facade behind which it hides the human body together with its fragility and vicissitudes. The "extraordinary body" (Thomson 1997a) is revealed in even the most "ordinary of bodies" and disability is indicative not only of this but also of the disruption that would lay bare the "whole underside of appearances" as well as the "extraordinary secret" buried deep within the ordinary.

Living among others as an individual is, as Stiker suggests, an impossibility for disabled people. As much as we are like everyone else, we are only like them. This alikeness goes far beyond the individual; it is reflective of a commitment to ordinariness as a representation of what life, both individual and collective, ought to be. Disability mirrors this to nondisability. The likeness of the one is Other. Any difference can be ignored and avoided if it bears the likeness of the one doing the ignoring and avoiding. A disabled person is granted individual status only in the act of mirroring such status—only in the act of mimesis. Stiker is right: disabled people are "good to worry about." Lévi-Strauss is partially right: disabled people are "good to think about." A little push, and he would have been all the way right: disabled people are "good to think with." The mimetic character of disability ought to evoke both thought and worry.

Mimesis and Disability

Thinking and worrying about disability comes fairly natural to contemporary society. This thinking does not, as Lennard Davis (1997, 2) suggests, encompass the sense of wonder and awe found in the ancient Greek sense of *Theoria*. The contemporary thinking about disability is not borne of the *aporia* that engenders the interrogation of what it means to be human both individually and collectively. Instead, this thinking is more mechanical (Michalko 1998) and thus leads to a pragmatic and instrumental understanding of disability. This thinking generates questions about how to prevent disability, how to cure it, and what to do with it when it cannot be either, and this is what contemporary society worries about in relation to disability.

But, there is another, very different reason to worry about disability. Disabled people, particularly since the advent of the disability movement and Disability Studies, are themselves beginning both to think and to worry about the ways in which society has been doing such thinking and worrying. Thinking and worrying about disability and its subsequent programmatics has been going on for a long time without disabled people, leading disabled theorists such as James Charlton (1998) to proclaim "Nothing about us without us." Even though this exclusion still continues, it is becoming more difficult to sustain it. Government agencies and other institutions designed to "help" disabled people are now being forced to listen to what disabled people think and worry about. How serious these agencies and institutions are in this endeavor is certainly debatable, but that they are taking disabled peoples' concerns into account, at least to some degree, is borne out by the recent introduction of legislation that responds to the rights of disabled people. In fact, the discussions surrounding such legislation provides the "new worry" for society; what do we do now that they think they have rights? How are we supposed to help them if they want "no pity" (Shapiro 1993)? What are we supposed to do with those

Deaf people who do not want cochlear implants and do not want to hear again? What do we do in our universities when some disabled academics think that Disability Studies is a legitimate academic pursuit?

These are very different kinds of worries than those to which society is accustomed. But worrying about what to do with disability conceived of as a question of rights or what to do with "no pity" or what to do with Disability Studies should not be confused with a concern for these issues. A genuine concern for these issues, something that necessarily goes beyond worrying, means that society would have to join with disabled people in the movement (both political and academic) to transform disability from an individual phenomenon to a sociopolitical one. Only with such a transformation could the "new worries" about disability be transformed into genuine concern.

A genuine concern requires a different kind of thinking about disability than the customary and dominant mechanical version. Everyone, including every society, has practical issues that require practical solutions and disability is no different. Disabled people (like everyone else) have many practical things to do and must find ways (often different from nondisabled ways) to do them, and this is what makes them "like everyone else." But, this practicality, while being part of disability, is not the whole of it. Yet, this is what contemporary society does with disability—*it confuses the part for the whole.*

In order to recover disability as something to think with rather than about, it is necessary to understand that how society conceives of, interprets, and treats its disabled members tells us more about our society than it does about its individual disabled members. To this extent, disability is mimetic. It acts as a mirror for society. Society is reflected in disability in terms of how society interprets disability.

It is important now to take a "closer look" at the connection between mimesis and disability. In his study of mimesis, Michael Taussig (1993, 19) says, "The ability to mime and mime well . . . is the capacity to Other." In my days of passing I drew on my mimetic quality with its ability to mime well. This mimetic exercise relied upon my childhood experience of being sighted as well as upon my later understanding that this childhood experience could be interactionally and strategically employed to imitate sight now that I was legally blind. I "saw" sight as a series of interactional accomplishments and, through mime, I could imitate it. I employed the "language of sight," using visual metaphor in the implicitly expert way that everyone else did. My engagement with the world was also with my body. I moved my body—my eyes, my hands, my legs and arms—with the intention of imitating someone who moved in the midst of seeing and sights. I "walked the walk and talked the talk" that was sightedness.

What else was I engaged in if not Othering? What I was Othering, however, is not so straightforward. Clearly, my passing depicted sightedness as Other, but it also depicted my blindness in the same way. I could not imitate sightedness unless it were Other and thus some thing to be imitated. But, what of my blindness? Where was it during all of my imitating? Any imitation, to be successful, must disguise the fact that it is not real—it must disguise the fact that it is not the thing being imitated. My disguise (sightedness) revealed blindness as something essentially different and Other to me. In my imitation, I Othered not only sightedness but blindness as well! My identity floated somewhere in that nebulous region of the Between (Titchkosky 1997, 2001) in the liminal space (Murphy et al. 1988) bordered by sightedness on one side and blindness on the other. I was both and neither.

From the liminal space between blindness and sightedness, I replicated sightedness and, in so doing, I constituted an identity that exercised some power over both blindness and sightedness.

> Note the *replicas*. Note the magical, the soulful power that derives from replication. For this is where we must begin; with the magical power of replication, the image affecting what it is an image of, wherein the representation shares in or takes power from the represented—testimony to the power of the mimetic faculty through whose awakening we might not so much understand that shadow of science known as magic (a forlorn task if ever there was one), but see anew the spell of the natural where the reproduction of life merges with the recapture of the soul. (Taussig 1993, 2)

The replication of which I am speaking and that which concerns Michael Taussig are certainly different. Still, there are similarities; whereas Taussig is interested in glimpsing that "shadow of science known as magic," I am interested in glimpsing that shadow of sight known as reality. Taussig's interest in his replicas and my interest in mine share the commitment of seeing "anew the spell of the natural." There is something magical about this—both in Taussig's study and in my passing. My passing represented sightedness and, in that, it shared in and took power from the represented. As philosophy has repeatedly told us, sight can see many things, but it cannot see itself—sight cannot see itself seeing. In imitating (replicating) sight, I was compelled (Thomson 1996, xvii) by the "spell of nature" and at the same time I shared in (took) its power in affecting an "image of reality." I also took from the power of sight insofar as I tricked ("magic"?) sight into seeing me as an instance of itself.

The modern version of the "natural" presents nature as a ubiquitous and thus essential feature of life, including human life. Nature is everywhere and in everything, as the contemporary revitalization of biological determinism attests. "Seeing nature" in everyone and in everything is what provides for the possibility of "norming" (Davis 1995) human life but only under the "spell of nature," yielding a "naturalized humanity." So strong is this spell that any naturalized version of humanity sees nothing other and through no other lens than the "natural." The modern version of humanity as natural *is itself an imitation* of its own conception of nature. The act of norming is one such imitation—it is modernity's attempt to mime nature, although it does not mime very well.

This "natural inclination" to norm human life is what provides for the possibility of seeing any impairment as biology gone wrong. It also provides the impetus for seeing disabled people within the contemporary dichotomy of the heroic and the tragic. Those of us who adjust to our impairments—which means those of us who conceive of our impairments biologically and do our best to "fit in"—induce praise from our society, praise for even the doing of the most insignificant things such as eating a meal or crossing a street. The doing of such things makes us heroic. Those of us who do not adjust and do not do these things, in contrast, are tragic, understandably so, but tragic. Even nature has its casualties. But, the heroic is the modern version of mimesis. Disabled people are heroic so long as we imitate the natural and the norm through our display of a commitment to it. So long as we act as if we are "normal people," albeit with an "abnormal biology," and so long as we adjust to this biology and do things, albeit differently, we are heroic. Disabled people are expected to imitate the natural and the norm and are expected to "see" our disabilities as biological conditions attached to a "natural, normal person."

Adjustment and doing things differently is, to borrow from Taussig, the "reproduction of life." In doing things differently—in being like everyone else—disabled people are often viewed as reproducing natural and normal life. Disability is mimetic insofar as it mirrors (recaptures) the "soul," as Taussig puts it, of this life. The tragic side of disability is captured in the nondisability standpoint that disability is a reminder, as Davis (1997, 2) suggests, of the fragility of the human body. Its heroic side, again from the same standpoint, reminds nondisability of the power of the natural, normal person to adjust to the conditions of life. The more successfully disabled people can mime the natural and the normal, the more and the clearer can the "world of the normal" see itself in disability.

There is still another and, more important, way in which disability is mimetic. Miming the natural can also be empowering. "Yet the important point about what I call the magic of mimeses is the same—namely that 'in some way or another' the making and existence of the artifact that portrays something gives one power over that which is portrayed" (Taussig 1993, 13). My passing as sighted during adolescence was, to borrow from Garfinkel 1967, an accomplishment, a production, an achievement, a construction of sightedness. I "built" sight out of the building blocks of my cultural apparatus. I used language, gestures, memories, and all other forms of interactional strategies as a means to imitate "natural seeing." The "magic of mimesis" was that I could produce an artifact (an imitation) of sight—something that everyone else implicitly conceived of as belonging to the powerful realm of nature. That I could imitate sight and be taken as an instance of it gave me at least some intuitive sense of the hubris involved in the power and spell of nature. While I was under the spell of nature—thinking that the only good life was the sighted life—I was able to cast my own spell over nature and to intuitively grasp, in an adolescent way, that the power-of-seeing (nature) resided in an unreflexive human understanding of nature. This intuition was certainly underdeveloped during my teenage years of passing. Seeing was "natural and good," my imitation of it was nothing more than second best. Still, this adolescent intuition served me well in my later and retrospective formulation of nature as bound by the spell of human imaginings and interpretation.

Yet, there is something more to the mimetic quality with its propensity to imitate—something more than the straightforward desire to be the Other and, in imitation, to have power over it. There is also something more in the imitations themselves—something more to marvel at than the fidelity of the replica or the representation. "Seeing resemblances seems so cerebral, a cognitive affair with the worldly. How on earth, then, could it be the rudiment of 'nothing other' than a 'compulsion,' let alone a compulsion to actually be the Other?" (Taussig 1993, 33). There is no doubt that the "world of the normal" is indeed compelling and even seductive, as Rosemarie Garland Thomson (1996, xvii) says, to disabled people. Passing as one of this world's "normal members" is certainly compelling, as it was for me during my teens, and is unequivocally an activity born of seduction by this world. I also marveled at my various replicas of sightedness—cerebral though this marveling was.

But, as Taussig suggests, resembling sightedness goes far beyond, and includes more, than passing. It is also born of more than the compelling and seductive character of the "world of the normal" and of the compulsion to be the Other. The compulsion—if it is so—to imitate "normal life" without concealing disability is born of something other than the compulsion to be the Other. Thomson (1996, xvii), a very visibly disabled woman, comes out as disabled and I, very "visibly blind," still pass! We move in the "world of the normal" acting as if we belong there.

What can we make of this somewhat unusual situation? I teach at a university alongside nondisabled others, and so does Thomson. I do what they do—I teach, grade exams, write books—and so does Thomson. Still, I pass: I move through the university like everyone else; I move through it acting as though the world, including me, is "seeable" by everyone, including me—if I could see. Yet, I move through the university differently from nondisabled others. I move with a guide dog, they do not; I ask my sociology students how they recognize both themselves and others as people who "see"; I ask my students to "walk" around the university with an "eye" to "see" the type of person the architecture and artifice of the university intended and expected to have show up. I tell my students not to raise their hands in class to let me know they want to ask a question.

In the midst of all this difference am I still passing, am I still imitating anything? Being very visibly disabled, is Thomson "coming out" as disabled? What are we doing? Or better, what are we representing, replicating, and imitating? We are certainly "doing things differently" from nondisabled others, but we are also "coming out" as disabled. We are "carving out an identity," as Thomson (1997a, 114) says, in the midst of the doing of things, but an identity steeped in disability. I do things, but no longer to prove that I can and no longer to pass as sighted. I do things "like everyone else"—I do them because I am a blind professor.

The compulsion to imitate nondisability through the doing of things is no longer the compulsion to be the Other. This compulsion is now borne from a compelling and seductive need to be a professor, to be a lawyer, to be a mother, to be. . . . It is the compulsion to be these things, disabled.

What disabled people can be "seen" to imitate, in our various ways, is belongingness. There is no "natural place" for us in the "world of the normal." Instead, this world makes a few adjustments (accommodations) such as wheelchair ramps, Braille markings on elevator pads, and special education programs, thereby fitting (including) us in. But when we "come out" as disabled, we begin to make a place for disability. Our compulsion to make a place for disability is concretized through imitating belongingness and acting "as if" we belong "in the world of the normal."

The sense of belonging, not the mere doing of things, generates the need and compulsion to make a place for disability. "Thinking with" disability instead of "about it" recommends that we "think through"

(disturb?) those places ready-made—usually by nondisabled others—
for disabled people. Interrogating and thus disturbing the places that
society makes for disabled people tells us more about society and its
conception of disability than it does about disability itself. Coming out
as disabled is a process whereby collective representations of disability
are "outed" and this is often disturbing.

Imitating belongingness replicates and thus produces an image of
society together with its rhetoric and practices of humanity. Disabled
people—through coming out, through the disability movement, and
through Disability Studies—imitate belongingness and thus produce a
replica of society's version of human rights, participation and thus a
version of the type of member that society typifies as having the right
of access to participation. This is often a disturbing sight (site) to society. First, it disturbs by depicting the often tacit set of socially constructed criteria for "right to membership" and for normalcy. Second,
it disturbs by invoking an epistemological "standpoint of disability"
through the social process of imitating belongingness. Society is disturbed by any marginal group that claims collective status (minoritiza-
tion) as a standpoint while simultaneously imitating a belongingness to
the "world of the center."

The mimesis of disability with its imitation of belongingness, is not
for appropriation. The appropriation of this imitation as "really center"
by nondisability cannot be totally affected by its own production of
likenesses constructed through such rituals as people-first language.
Society, the "god of normalcy" (Durkheim 1915), worshipped through
the ritualized production of normate culture, cannot be sustained when
disability comes out. The appropriation of this coming out by normate
culture does not recognize its own mimetic character, let alone that of
disability. "There is a premium on establishing the capacity to see from
the peripheries and the depths. But here lies a serious danger of ro-
manticizing and/or appropriating the vision of the less powerful while
claiming to see from their positions. To see from below is neither easily learned nor unproblematic, even if 'we' 'naturally' inhabit the great
underground terrain of subjugated knowledges" (Haraway 1998, 193).
The epistemological standpoint of disability is a premium for both

disability and nondisability. The imitations that flow from such a standpoint should not be romanticized or appropriated and neither should they be reified. We, disabled people, need to learn, difficult as it is, that living between and among imitations permits a "vision" from the "great underground terrain of subjugated knowledges." This permits for replicating belongingness *through* coming out as disabled. The compulsion to imitate nondisability is the quintessential "impediment" imposed on disabled people by either nondisabled people or ourselves. It impedes any life in the underground terrain of subjugated knowledges and it impedes any disturbance to the reification of normate culture. The life and the knowledge of the underground terrain lived in the space of betweenness mimes the life and the knowledge above ground.

Let us suffer this inquestive demand that is the place of disability— let us come out and meet there.

Notes

Chapter One

1. See, for example, Corker and French 1999b; Davis 1995, 1997; Gadacz 1994; Linton 1998; Mitchell and Snyder 1997; Oliver 1996; Shakespeare 1998; Thomson 1997a.

2. For an excellent analysis of a variety of definitions of disability, their interpretation and their consequences for the lives of disabled people, see Wendell 1996, 11–34.

Chapter Two

1. An interesting corollary: recently (decades after this-name calling incident) I was speaking with a female colleague. She is untenured and new to the faculty. We were discussing the controversy in which she was recently involved. A group of students at the university wanted a motion passed at Senate. The motion was so controversial that no tenured professors would make it. The students asked my colleague and, despite her untenured status, she took the risk and made the motion. Students admired her for her action and she soon acquired a reputation around the university. While we were talking, a male student walked by, turned around and, taking a few steps closer to us, said to my colleague, "You've got balls." Male organ-izing of the feminine is alive and well to this day.

2. Much has been written about the connection between disability and genetics. See Parens and Asch 1999 for an excellent review of this connection and McVicar 2001 for an excellent interpretation of its social significance in terms of the creation and uncreation of societal conceptions of worthwhile members.

3. The distinction here is between deaf, referring to the physical impairment of not hearing or not hearing well and Deaf which refers to a culture with its own language. See Corker 1998; Lane, Hoffmeister, and Bahan 1996.

4. The only nonscientific version of experiencing genetics comes through commonsense accounts of familial connection. "She has her father's nose," "He's

177

got his mother's eyes," "The apple doesn't fall far from the tree," "She comes by it naturally" are but a few examples of such accounts.

5. I am not raising Frank's work here as a way to suggest that illness and disability are the same. Instead, I raise it in order to further interrogate the metaphysics of the *Why me?* question as it relates to current biological conceptions of life.

Chapter Three

1. For a review of such criticism, see Imrie 1996, 27–50. It is instructive to read this critique along with Darke's review (1998) of Imrie's work. For another review of the social model, see Marks 1999, especially chap. 4. Shildrick and Price 1996 provides a reading of the social model's construction of the body. Corker and French 1999a discusses "oppression" and the way in which the social model conceives of it. Corker 1999 compares the social model with the work of Simi Linton. See also Tom Shakespeare and Nicholas Watson's "defence" (1997) of the social model and Ruth Pinder's reply (1997). Oliver (1996, 30–42) himself addresses criticism of his work regarding the social model. With few exceptions (see Corker 1999; Shildrick and Price 1996) the criticisms of the social model seem to focus on its limited "explanation" of disability experience as well as its limitation in "accounting" for disability experience. Whether or not the social model "empirically" corresponds to a positivist version of experience is not my interest here. I am more interested in its implicit understandings of the body.

Chapter Four

1. An exception to this is the work of Georg Simmel (see Stewart 1999). For recent examples, see Featherstone, Hepworth, and Turner 1991; Frank 1995; Howes 1991; O'Neil 1985; Shilling 1993; Synnott 1993; Turner 1996. For an excellent review of this development of the interest in the body see Frank 1990. However, various feminisms are arguably the chief originators of such an interest. See Bordo 1993; Butler 1993; Smith 1987, 1990, 1999; Wendell 1996.

2. I am referring here to the postmodern contention that social reality is bereft of origin and essence and consists only of image. Of course, postmodernism privileges vision and the visual image.

3. I follow the work of Drew Leder. He suggests that when the body is working properly it "disappears." Leder 1990, 83–84, contrasts this with the dysappearance of the nonworking body, "that is, the body *appears* as thematic focus, but precisely in a *dys* state." I am suggesting that when eyes "do not work," not only do they represent Leder's sense of dysappearance but the appearances of the world are also "dysappearance"—they too are in a dys-state. This, of course, comes about only when the body is conceived instrumentally, "as a tool."

4. Since Smokie's death, I have a new blindness—one with a white cane as my guide. Yet, I still talk to Smokie, silently now, as I move through the world. It

seems as though there is more to figure out now, probably because the cane can never replace Smokie's guidance.

5. I rely heavily on Canguilhem 1991 and Merleau-Ponty 1962 for what follows. The concept "normal human biology" is not as simple and as neutral as it appears. For an excellent analysis of how this concept fluctuates in the ongoing dialectic of normalcy/abnormalcy and of how the biological and medical sciences invoke the tacit sense of "typical functioning" as a way to privilege normal human biology as natural, see Silvers 1998.

6. For an excellent discussion about the modern version of the environment as "neutral," see Sennett 1990, especially pages 41–68. Distortion is located in the subject since the object (environment) is neutral.

7. This sardonic and even flippant micro analysis of the development (techniques) of a self and of the social identity "disability" reveals a macro development of such a self and of such an identity. Michel Foucault (1978) provides the basis for a macro analysis in his understanding of governmental transformations of "people" into "populations." "Movements of life," (25) such as disability, are thus transformed into rates as well as into a population with rights. But such a transformation brings with it a version of a "disabled self" (social identity) that must conform to surveillance and to the proof that one belongs in this population, thereby having rights. Such an analysis is beyond the scope of this book since my intention is to unravel the phenomenological dilemma of suffering that presents itself in the face of disability. It is necessary for this sort of analysis to be conducted in order to reveal the governmental and institutional "techniques" involved in the development of a Self.

8. I rely heavily on Enns 1999 in the following discussion. My point in this section is not to provide a descriptive account of the Latimer case but to explicate the social consequences of understanding disability as useless-difference.

Chapter Five

1. In raising illness, my intention is not to blur the distinction between disability and illness. These categories are distinct and medicalizing disability does blur the distinction. See, for example, Oliver 1990, 49–54. My aim here is to develop the idea of disability through Lacan's notions of the Real and Imaginary and to show disability as narrative.

Chapter Six

1. For excellent examples of such accounts, see Davis 1995; Mitchell and Snyder 1997; Russell 1998; Stiker 1999; Thomson 1997a. It is important to note, however, that like anything else, disability is a historical phenomenon. For example, even though I address the phenomenon of suffering as it relates to disability and try to show the social character of such a relation, suffering and disability are historically connected. (See the sources above.) The contemporary connection

between suffering and disability is embedded in the historical movement of Western society. Such a connection may be analyzed for other societies as well.

2. The (my) act of passing can be interpreted as a version of what Lauren Berlant (1997) calls "infantile citizenship." Berlant suggests that the achievement of such a citizenship confirms that "nation" (in my case, the "naturally seeing world") exists and that "we are in it," that I can act as if I belong (50). Despite my "active" passing, I conducted myself "as if" I had no choice—it is natural to see—and thus, like Berlant's infantile citizen, my action was bereft of agency, the action of "normal-style citizens of zero-sum mnemonic, a default consciousness of the nation with no imagination of agency" (50). I develop the idea of mimesis later in this chapter.

References

Abberley, Paul. 1987. "The Concept of Oppression and the Development of a Social Theory of Disability." *Disability, Handicap, and Society* 2(1): 5–19.

Arendt, Hannah. 1955. *Men in Dark Times*. San Diego: Harcourt Brace Jovanovich.

———. 1958. *The Human Condition*. Chicago: University of Chicago Press.

———. 1963. *Eichmann in Jerusalem: A Report on the Banality of Evil*. New York: Penguin.

Bakhtin, Mikhail Mikhailovich. 1986. Edited by Caryl Emerson and Michael Holquist. Translated by Vern W. McGee. *Speech Genres and Other Late Essays*. Austin: University of Texas Press.

Bakker, J. I. 1999. Review of Rod Michalko's "The Eye and the Shadow of Blindness." *Canadian Review of Sociology and Anthropology* 36(2): 305–6.

Barnes, Colin. 1996. "Visual Impairment and Disability." In *Beyond Disability: Towards an Enabling Society*, edited by Gerald Hales. Thousand Oaks, Calif.: Sage. 37–44.

———. 1998. "The Social Model of Disability: A Sociological Phenomenon Ignored by Sociologists?" In *The Disability Reader: Social Science Perspectives*, edited by Tom Shakespeare. New York: Cassell Academic. 66–78.

Barthes, Roland. 1982. *Mythologies*. Paris: Editions du Seuil, 1957. Translated by Annette Lavers. London: Granada.

Baudrillard, Jean. 1981. *For a Critique of the Political Economy of the Sign*. Translated by Charles Levin. New York: Telos.

———. 1990. *Seduction*. Translated by Brian Singer. Montreal: New World Perspectives.

Beck, Ulrich. 1992. *Risk Society: Towards a New Modernity*. Translated by Mark Ritter. Newbury Park, Calif.: Sage.

Berlant, Lauren. 1997. *The Queen of America Goes to Washington City: Essays on Sex and Citizenship*. Durham, N.C.: Duke University Press.

Bickenbach, Jerome. 1993. *Physical Disability and Social Policy*. Toronto: University of Toronto Press.

Bordo, Susan. 1993. *Unbearable Weight: Feminism, Western Culture, and the Body*. Berkeley and Los Angeles: University of California Press.

Butler, Judith. 1993. *Bodies That Matter.* New York: Routledge.

Canada. Federal, Provincial, and Territorial Ministers Responsible for Social Services. 1998. *In Unison: A Canadian Approach to Disability Issues.* Vision paper. Hull.

Canguilhem, Georges. 1991. Reprint. *The Normal and the Pathological.* Translated by Carolyn R. Fawcett in collaboration with Robert S. Cohen. With an Introduction by Michel Foucault. New York: Zone Books. Original edition, *Le Normal and le pathologique.* Paris: Presses Universitaires de France, 1966.

Charlton, James I. 1998. *Nothing about Us without Us.* Berkeley and Los Angeles: University of California Press.

Cooley, Charles Horton. 1909. *Social Organization.* New York: Schocken Books.

Corker, Mairian. 1998. "Disability Discourse in a Postmodern World." In *The Disability Reader: Social Science Perspectives,* edited by Tom Shakespeare. New York: Cassell Academic. 221–33.

———. 1999. "New Disability Discourse: The Principle of Optimization and Social Change." In *Disability Discourse,* edited by Mairian Corker and Sally French. Philadelphia: Open University Press. 192–209.

Corker, Mairian, and Sally French. 1999a. "Reclaiming Discourse in Disability Studies." In *Disability Discourse,* edited by Mairian Corker and Sally French. Philadelphia: Open University Press. 1–11.

———, eds. 1999b. *Disability Discourse.* Philadelphia: Open University Press.

Crawford, Robert. 1980. "Healthism and the Medicalization of Everyday Life." *Journal of Health and Sciences* 10(3): 365–88.

Darke, Anthony. 1998. "Review of Rob Imrie, *Disability and the City.*" *Sociology* 32(1): 223–34.

Davis, Fred. 1961. "Deviance Disavowal: The Management of Strained Interaction by the Visibly Handicapped." *Social Problems* 9:120–32.

Davis, Ken. 1996. "Disability and Legislation: Rights and Equality." In *Beyond Disability: Towards an Enabling Society,* edited by Gerald Hales. Thousand Oaks, Calif.: Sage Publications. 124–33.

Davis, Lennard J. 1995. *Enforcing Normalcy: Disability, Deafness, and the Body.* London: Verso.

———. 1997. "The Need for Disability Studies." In *The Disability Studies Reader,* edited by Lennard J. Davis. New York: Routledge. 1–6.

"Don." 2000. Interview by author. Tape recording. Vancouver, B.C., March.

Durkheim, Emile. 1915. *The Elementary Forms of Religious Life.* New York: Free Press.

Dyer, Richard. 1993. *The Matter of Images: Essays on Representations.* New York: Routledge.

Eckstein, Cheryl. 1995. "Tracy Latimer, Better Off Dead? A Breach of Compassion." Compassionate Healthcare Network, March. http://www.chninternational.com/tracybod.htm

Enns, Ruth. 1999. *A Voice Unheard: The Latimer Case and People with Disabilities.* Halifax: Fernwood.

Father. 1999. Interview by author. Tape recording. Halifax, October.

————. 2000. Interview by author. Tape recording. Toronto, April.

Featherstone, Mike, Mike Hepworth, and Bryan S. Turner, eds. 1991. *The Body: Social Process and Cultural Theory.* Newbury Park, Calif.: Sage.

Foster, Hal, ed. 1988. *Vision and Visuality: Discussions in Contemporary Culture.* Seattle: Bay Press.

Foucault, Michel. 1978. *The History of Sexuality. Volume 1, An Introduction.* Translated by Robert Hurley. New York: Vintage.

————. 1979. *Discipline and Punish: The Birth of the Prison.* Translated by Alan Sheridan. New York: Vintage.

————. 1980. *Power/Knowledge: Selected Interviews and Other Writings, 1972–1977.* Edited by Colin Gordon. Translated by Colin Gordon, Leo Marshall, John Mepham, and Kate Soper. New York: Pantheon.

Frank, Arthur W. 1990. "Bringing Bodies Back In: A Decade Review." *Theory, Culture, and Society* 7(1): 131–62.

————. 1991. *At the Will of the Body: Reflections on Illness.* Boston: Houghton Mifflin.

————. 1994. "Reclaiming an Orphan Genre: The First-Person Narrative of Illness." *Literature and Medicine* 13(1): 1–21.

————. 1995. *The Wounded Story Teller: Body, Illness, and Ethics.* Chicago: University of Chicago Press.

————. 1998. "From Dysappearance to Hyperappearance: Sliding Boundaries of Illness and Bodies." *The Body and Psychology.* Edited by Henderikus J. Stam. London: Sage. 205–32.

Gadacz, René R. 1994. *Re-Thinking Dis-Ability: New Structures, New Relationships.* Edmonton: University of Alberta Press.

Gadamer, Hans-Georg. 1975. *Truth and Method.* New York: Crossroad.

Garfinkel, Harold. 1967. *Studies in Ethnomethodology.* Englewood Cliffs, N. J.: Prentice-Hall.

Gartner, Alan, and Tom Joe, eds. 1987. *Images of the Disabled, Disabling Images.* New York: Praeger.

Goffman, Erving. 1959. *The Presentation of Self in Everyday Life.* New York: Doubleday Anchor.

————. 1963. *Stigma: Notes on the Management of Spoiled Identity.* Englewood Cliffs, N. J.: Prentice-Hall.

Haraway, Donna. 1998. "The Persistence of Vision." In *The Visual Culture Reader,* edited by Nicholas Mirzoeff. New York: Routledge. 191–98.

Harrison, Felicity, and Mary Crow. 1993. *Living and Learning with Blind Children: A Guide for Parents and Teachers of Visually Impaired Children.* Toronto: University of Toronto Press.

Heidegger, Martin. 1962. *Being and Time.* Translated by John Macquarrie and Edward Robinson. New York: Harper & Row.

Hobbes, Thomas. 1958. *Leviathan: Parts I and II.* Edited by Herbert W. Schneider. Indianapolis: Bobbs-Merrill.

Howes, David, ed. 1991. *The Variety of Sensory Experience: A Sourcebook in the Anthropology of the Senses.* Toronto: University of Toronto Press.

Hubbard, Ruth. 1997. "Abortion and Disability." In *The Disability Studies Reader*, edited by Lennard J. Davis. New York: Routledge. 187–200.

Hughes, Bill, and Kevin Paterson. 1997. "The Social Model of Disability and the Disappearing Body: Towards a Sociology of Impairment." *Disability and Society* 12(3): 325–40.

Imrie, Rob. 1996. *Disability and the City: International Perspectives*. New York: St. Martin's Press.

Ingstad, Benedicte, and Susan Reynolds Whyte, eds. 1995. *Disability and Culture*. Berkeley and Los Angeles: University of California Press.

Jay, Martin. 1994. *Downcast Eyes: The Denigration of Vision in Twentieth-Century French Thought*. Berkeley and Los Angeles: University of California Press.

Jenks, Chris, ed. 1995. *Visual Culture*. New York: Routledge.

Karatheodoris, Stephen. 1982. "Blindness, Illusion, and the Need for an Image of Sight." *Reflections: Canadian Journal of Visual Impairment* 1:31–51.

Kleinman, Arthur, Veena Das, and Margaret Lock, eds. 1997. *Social Suffering*. Berkeley and Los Angeles: University of California Press.

Kleinman, Arthur, and Joan Kleinman. 1997. "The Appeal of Experience; the Dismay of Images: Cultural Appropriations of Suffering in Our Times." In *Social Suffering*, edited by Arthur Kleinman, Veena Das, and Margaret Lock. Berkeley and Los Angeles: University of California Press. 1–24.

Klobas, Lauri E. 1988. *Disability Drama in Television and Film*. Jefferson, N.C.: McFarlan.

Kuhn, Thomas S. 1962. *The Structure of Scientific Revolutions*. Chicago: University of Chicago Press.

Lacan, Jacques. 1968. *Speech and Language in Psychoanalysis*. Translated by Anthony Wilden. Baltimore, Md.: Johns Hopkins University Press.

———. 1977. *Ecrits: A Selection*. Translated by Alan Sheridan. New York: Tavistock.

Lane, Harlan, Robert Hoffmeister, and Ben Bahan. 1996. *A Journey into the Deaf-World*. San Diego: Dawn Sign Press.

Leder, Drew. 1990. *The Absent Body*. Chicago: University of Chicago Press.

Levin, David Michael. 1988. *The Opening of Vision: Nihilism and the Postmodern Situation*. New York: Routledge.

Levinas, Emmanuel. 1969. *Totality and Infinity: An Essay on Exteriority*. Translated by Alphonso Lingis. Pittsburgh, Pa. Duquesne University Press.

———. 1988. "Useless Suffering." Translated by Richard Cohen. In *The Provocation of Levinas: Rethinking the Other*, edited by Robert Bernasconi and David Wood. New York: Routledge. 156–67.

Linton, Simi. 1998. *Claiming Disability: Knowledge and Identity*. New York: New York University Press.

Macnaughten, Phil, and John Urry. 1995. "Towards a Sociology of Nature." *Sociology* 29:203–20.

Magee, Bryan, and Martin Milligan. 1995. *On Blindness: Letters between Bryan Magee and Martin Milligan*. Oxford: Oxford University Press.

Mairs, Nancy. 1996. *Waist-High in the World: A Life among the Nondisabled*. Boston: Beacon Press.

Marks, Deborah. 1999. *Disability: Controversial Debates and Psychosocial Perspectives*. New York: Routledge.

McVicar, Lindsay. 2001. "The Push to Know: Technology and the Discourse of Reproductive Certainty." Sociology honors thesis, St. Francis Xavier University, Antigonish, N.S.

Mead, George Herbert. 1934. *Mind, Self, and Society from the Standpoint of a Social Behaviorist*. Edited by Charles W. Morris. Chicago: University of Chicago Press.

Merleau-Ponty, Maurice. 1962. *Phenomenology of Perception*. Translated by Colin Smith. New York: Humanities.

Michalko, Rod. 1982. "Accomplishing a Sighted World." *Reflections: Canadian Journal of Visual Impairment* 1:9–30.

———. 1984. "The Metaphor of Adolescence." *Phenomenology and Pedagogy* 1(3): 296–311.

———. 1987. "The Birth of Disability" *Phenomenology and Pedagogy* 5(2): 119–131.

———. 1998. *The Mystery of the Eye and the Shadow of Blindness*. Toronto: University of Toronto Press.

———. 1999. *The Two-in-One: Walking with Smokie, Walking with Blindness*. Philadelphia: Temple University Press.

Michalko, Rod, and Tanya Titchkosky. 2001. "Putting Disability in Its Place: It's Not a Joking Matter." In *Embodied Rhetorics: Disability in Language and Culture*, edited by James C. Wilson and Cynthia Lewicki-Wilson. Carbondale: Southern Illinois University Press.

Mirzoeff, Nicholas, ed. 1998. *The Visual Culture Reader*. New York: Routledge.

Mitchell, David T., and Sharon L. Snyder. 1997. "Disability Studies and the Double Bind of Representation." In *The Body and Physical Difference: Discourses of Disability*, edited by Mitchell and Snyder. Ann Arbor: University of Michigan Press. 1–31.

Morris, Jenny. 1991. *Pride against Prejudice: Transforming Attitudes to Disability*. Philadelphia: New Society.

Murphy, R., J. Scheer, Y. Murphy, and R. Mack. 1988. "Physical Disability and Social Liminality: A Study in the Rituals of Adversity." *Social Science and Medicine* 26(2): 235–42.

Murphy, Robert. 1987. *The Body Silent*. New York: W. W. Norton.

Nietzsche, Friedrich. 1968. *The Will to Power*. Translated by Walter Kaufmann and R. J. Hollingdale. New York: Vintage.

Norden, Martin F. 1994. *The Cinema of Isolation: A History of Physical Disability in the Movies*. New Brunswick, N.J.: Rutgers University Press.

Oliver, Michael. 1990. *The Politics of Disablement: A Sociological Approach*. New York: St. Martin's.

———. 1996. *Understanding Disability: From Theory to Practice*. New York: St. Martin's.

Overboe, James. 1999. "'Difference in Itself': Validating Disabled People's Lived Experience." *Body and Society* 5(4): 17–29.

Parens, Erik, and Adrienne Asch. 1999. "The Disability Rights Critique of Prenatal Genetic Testing: Reflections and Recommendations." *Hastings Center Report*, September–October.

Parisian, Doug. 1981. *The Positive Path: Profiles of Disabled Manitobans.* Winnipeg: Hignell.

Pinder, Ruth. 1997. "A Reply to Tom Shakespeare and Nicholas Watson." *Disability and Society* 12(2): 301–5.

Robillard, Albert. 1999. *Meaning of a Disability: The Lived Experience of Paralysis.* Philadelphia: Temple University Press.

Rousseau, Jean-Jacques. 1968. *The Social Contract.* Translated by Maurice Cranston. Baltimore, Md.: Penguin.

Russell, Marta. 1998. *Beyond Ramps: Disability at the End of the Social Contract.* Monroe, Me.: Common Courage.

Said, Edward. 1990. "Reflections on Exile." In *Out There: Marginalization and Contemporary Culture*, edited by Russel Ferguson, Martha Gevner, Trinh T Minh-ha, and Cornel West. New York: New Museum of Contemporary Art; Cambridge, Mass.: MIT Press. 357–66.

Schutz, Alfred. 1973. *Collected Papers.* Volume 1, *The Problem of Social Reality.* Edited by Maurice Natanson. The Hague: Martinus Nijhoff.

Scott, Joan. 1995. "Multiculturalism and the Politics of Identity." In *The Identity in Question*, edited by John Rajchman. New York: Routledge. 3–12.

Sennett, Richard. 1990. *The Conscience of the Eye: The Design and Social Life of Cities.* New York: W. W. Norton.

Shakespeare, Tom, ed. 1998. *The Disability Reader: Social Science Perspectives.* New York: Cassell Academic.

Shakespeare, Tom, and Nicholas Watson. 1997. "Defending the Social Model." *Disability and Society* 12(2): 293–300.

Shapiro, Joseph P. 1993. *No Pity: People with Disabilities Forging a New Civil Rights Movement.* New York: Times Books.

Shildrick, Margrit, and Janet Price. 1996. "Breaking the Boundaries of the Broken Body." *Body and Society* 2(4): 93–113.

Shilling, Chris. 1993. *The Body and Social Theory.* Newbury Park, Calif.: Sage.

Shklar, Judith N. 1990. *The Faces of Injustice.* New Haven: Yale University Press.

Silvers, Anita. 1998. "A Fatal Attraction to Normalizing: Treating Disabilities as Deviations from "Species-Typical" Functioning." In *Enhancing Human Traits: Ethical and Social Implications*, edited by Erik Parens. Washington, D.C.: Georgetown University Press. 95–123.

Smith, Dorothy, E. 1987. *The Everyday World as Problematic: A Feminist Sociology.* Toronto: University of Toronto Press.

———. 1990. *The Conceptual Practices of Power: A Feminist Sociology of Knowledge.* Toronto: University of Toronto Press.

————. 1999. *Writing the Social: Critique, Theory, and Investigations.* Toronto: University of Toronto Press.

Stewart, Janet. 1999. "Georg Simmel at the Lectern: The Lecture as Embodiment of Text." *Body and Society* 5(4): 1–16.

Stiker, Henri-Jacques. 1999. *A History of Disability.* Translated by William Sayers. Ann Arbor: University of Michigan Press.

Susan. 2000. Interview by author. Tape recording. Montreal, April.

Synnott, Anthony. 1993. *The Body Social: Symbolism, Self, and Society.* New York: Routledge.

Taussig, Michael. 1993. *Mimesis and Alterity: A Particular History of the Senses.* New York: Routledge.

Taylor, Charles. 1989. *Sources of the Self: The Making of the Modern Identity.* Cambridge, Mass.: Harvard University Press.

Thomson, Rosemarie Garland. 1997a. *Extraordinary Bodies: Figuring Physical Disability in American Culture and Literature.* New York: Columbia University Press.

————. 1997b. "Feminist Theory, the Body, and the Disabled Figure." In *The Disability Studies Reader,* edited by Lennard J. Davis. New York: Routledge. 279–92.

————, ed. 1996. *Freakery: Cultural Spectacles of Extraordinary Body.* New York: New York University Press.

Titchkosky, Tanya. 1997. "The Primacy of Between-ness: Marginality and Art." Ph.D. dissertation, York University.

————. 1998. "Anorexia, Women, and Change." *Journal of Dharma* 23(4): 479–500.

————. 2000. "Disability Studies: Old or New?" *Canadian Journal of Sociology and Anthropology* 25(2): 197–224.

————. 2001. "Disability—A Rose By Any Other Name? People-First Language in Canadian Society." *Canadian Review of Sociology and Anthropology* 38(2): 125–40.

————. 2002. "Cultural Maps: Which Way to Disability?" In *Disability and Postmodernity: Embodying Disability Theory,* edited by Marian Corker and Tom Shakespeare. New York: Cassell Academic. 145–60.

————. n.d. "Disability Stays: An Introduction to the Social Construction of Disability." Typescript.

Turner, Bryan S. 1996. *The Body and Society: Explorations in Social Theory.* Thousand Oaks, Calif.: Sage.

Turner, Victor. 1985. *On the Edge of the Bush: Anthropology as Experience.* Edited by Edith L. B. Turner. Tucson: University of Arizona Press.

Weber, Max. 1947. *The Theory of Social and Economic Organization.* Translated by Talcott Parsons. New York: Free Press.

Wells, H. G. 1911. *"The Country of the Blind" and Other Stories.* London: T. Nelson.

Wendell, Susan. 1996. *The Rejected Body: Feminist Philosophical Reflections on Disability.* New York: Routledge.

West, Cornel. 1990. "The New Cultural Politics of Difference." In *Out There: Marginalization and Contemporary Cultures,* edited by Russel Ferguson, Martha

Gevner, Trinh T Minh-ha, and Cornel West. New York: New Museum of Contemporary Art; Cambridge, Mass.: MIT Press. 19–36.

———. 1995. "A Matter of Life and Death." In *The Identity in Question,* edited by John Rajchman. New York: Routledge. 15–32.

Williams, Gareth. 1998. "The Sociology of Disability: Towards a Materialist Phenomenology." In *The Disability Reader,* edited by Tom Shakespeare. New York: Cassell Academic. 234–44.

Zola, Irving Kenneth. 1977. "Healthism and Disabling Medicalization." In *Disabling Professions,* by Ivan Illich, Irving K. Zola, John McKnight, Jonathan Caplan, and Harley Shaiken. Salem, N.H.: M. Boyars.

———. 1982. *Missing Pieces: A Chronicle of Living with a Disability.* Philadelphia: Temple University Press.

———. 1988. "Whose Voice Is This Anyway?" *Medical Humanities Review* 2(1): 6–15.

———. 1991. "Bringing Our Bodies Back In: Reflections on a Past, Present, and Future Medical Society." *Journal of Health and Social Behaviour* 32 (March): 1–16.

———. 1993. "Self, Identity, and the Naming Question: Reflections on the Language of Disability." *Social Science and Medicine* 36(2): 167–73.

Index

Abberley, Paul, 56–58, 61
Abnormal/normal dichotomy, 23
Acceptance: of disability, 31; metaphysical questions on, 25–30
Accessibility, 127–30, 141; adult suffering and, 75–76; curb cuts for, 79, 163; environmental factors in, 141; experiences of, 20–21, 95–96; financial cost of, 15, 79, 164; guide dogs and, 2–4; lack of, 52, 55; minimalistic approach to, 129–30; of public transportation, 52, 79; ramps for, 173
Accident, as cause of disability, 5
Accommodating disability. See Accessibility
Accountability, 118
Activists, 21–22
Adaptations, 47; blindness and, 25; inclusion and, 163; individual approach to, 31; rehabilitation and, 31, 33, 140; technology and, 137, 163
Admiration for disabled persons, 12, 170–71
Adolescent experiences, 9–10, 20–23, 73–75, 149–50; and adult experiences compared, 75–76
Adult experiences, 75–81; and adolescent experiences compared, 75–76
Age, 60
Alienation, 73
Alternative health practices, 47
Amniocentesis, 65
Anthropological concepts, 75–77
Aphorisms, 23, 43
Architects, 129–30

Arendt, Hannah, 5, 19
Aspirations, adjustments to, 163
Assistive technology, 79–80; computer, 157; electronic magnification, 25
Attitudes: negative, 11–12, 81; positive, 161–62
Audio-recorded books, 9, 25

Barnes, Colin, 52–53, 75, 83
Barriers, environmental and social, 52. See also Accessibility
Barthes, Roland, 62, 69
Belonging, society and, 38–39, 128, 173–75
Benefits of disabilities, 27–29
Biofeedback, 47
Biomedicine, 6–7, 10, 13; ethics of, 99; metaphysical questions and, 30–36, 53; suffering and, 33–34. See also Natural body
Blame, 35
Blind persons: expected behavior of, 149; interviews with, 121–28
Blindisms, 137–39, 152
Blindness: definition of, 115–16; individual approach to, 22–23
Body: and connection to environment, 145; in interviews with blind persons, 123–28; knowledge of, 125; and mind-body connection, 35–36; societal conceptions of, 37
Books, audio-recorded, 9, 25
Braille, 163, 173
Building codes, 130–31

Canada: Charter of Rights and Freedoms in, 104; government reports from, 146–48
Cancer, personal experiences with, 35–36
Capitalist society, 57
Celebrations, 113
Cerebral palsy, 103, 109–10
Chaos, experience of, 131–32, 137
Charlton, James, 167
Charter of Rights and Freedoms (Canada), 104
Childhood experiences, 7–8, 149; parents and, 121, 135
Children: choosing to have, 41–42, 66; disabled, interviews with parents of, 121; ophthalmologists for, 121
Choosing disability, 13–16
Cochlear implants, 63, 168
Codes, building, 130–31
Collective identity: choosing disability and, 13–14; formation of, 6
Collective issues: impairment as, 60; marginalization, 22, 49; modes of experience, 65; normalcy and abnormalcy representations, 141; oppression, 52; ordinariness, 166; politics, 39
"Coming out": politics of, 70; rehabilitation and, 69–70
Community: exile from, 18; perceptions of, 18
Computer technology, assistive, 157
Conditions: disabling, 54; hereditary, 41–42
Consciousness: of disability, 83; political, 57
Costs: accessibility and, 15, 79, 164; government funding and, 162
Cultural image, 13–16, 24
Cultural representation, 1, 88
Culture: rituals of, 77–78; as source of disability, 141; Western, 1. See also Politics
Curb cuts, 79, 163
Cystic fibrosis, 134

Davis, Lennard, 44
Denial, 117
Descartes, René, 82
Dichotomy: abnormal/normal, 23; adolescence/adulthood, 75–76; equality/difference, 39; heroic/tragic, 170–71; normal/abnormal, 23; normal/pathological, 30–31; politics of, 23; subject/object, 84

Difference, 146–48; and equality compared, 39; and normalcy standard, 148–51; and ordinariness standard, 151–55; removal of, 148–55; useless, 93–103
Disability: activists, 21–22; biomedical reasons for, 30–36; causes of, 5, 54; choosing, 13–16; definition of, 51; and impairment compared, 52–53; incurable, 151; "medicalization" of, 53, 55; metaphysical reasons for, 25–30; rights, 96; scientific-rationalistic versions of, 133; source of, 113–41; studies on, 6, 14, 26, 167–68, 174
"Disability consciousness," 83
Disability Movement, 167–68
Disability Resource Centre, interviews in, 156–61
Disabling conditions, 54
Discrimination: individual, 4, 55, 153, 162–63; individual approach to, 52; institutional, 52
Disease, as cause of disability, 5, 54
"Distance sense," 124
Distortion, blindness and, 94
Dogs. See Guide dogs
Down syndrome, 65
Dysappearances, 85–87

Education: segregated, 52, 66; special, 66, 133, 173. See also Mainstreaming
Electronic magnification technology, 25
Encephalomyelitis, myalgic, 118
Enlightenment, 6, 108
Environment: barriers in, 52; blindness and, 90; connection to body and, 145; individual approach to, 141; social and physical, 127; as source of disability, 141. See also Accessibility; Society
Equality/difference dichotomy, 39
Ethics: biomedical, 99; of integration, 148; practical, 107, 110–11
Ethnicity, 60
Euthanasia, 45
Exclusion: caused by efforts to erase disability, 153, 167; from community, 18; experiences of, 20–21, 95–96; identity formation and, 15–16; through inaccessibility, 55, 130; inclusion as solution to, 144–46; from public places, 4, 11; segre-

gated education and, 52, 66. *See also* Inclusion

Exile. *See* Exclusion

Expectations, adjustments to, 163

Expressions, common, 43; blindness and, 23

Extraordinariness, 166

Eye charts, Snellen, 114, 115

Eye pigmentation, 8, 92

Faith, 165

Fear of disability, 11–12

Films, disabled represented in, 12, 24, 68

Financial costs: accessibility and, 15, 79, 164; government funding, 162

Finger, Anne, 61–62, 63, 65–67, 71

Fluidity, of disability, 116

Food distribution, 57

Frank, Arthur, 35–36, 128, 131–32, 140

Frustration, 64

Funding, government, 162

Gadacz, René, 127

Gender, 60

Geneticists, examinations by, 32–33

Genetic ophthalmologist, 66–67; first examination by, 117; on procreation, 41–43, 45–46, 48–50

Genetics: choosing parenthood and, 41–42; examinations and, 32–33; flawed, 5, 32–33, 45; identity formation and, 8; randomness of, 46; self-identity and, 32–33; society and, 22; testing in, 41

Genetic testing, 41

Government: Canadian, reports from, 146–48; funding, 162. *See also* Legislation

Greco-Roman ethos, 28

Guide dogs: accessibility and, 2–4; experiences with, 95; normalcy and, 79, 173; and passing as sighted, 149; relationship with, 15; and "world of appearances," 85

Healthism, 47

Health practices, alternative, 47

Hephaestus, 164–65

Hereditary conditions, 41–42, 63. *See also* Genetics

Heroic/tragic dichotomy, 170–71

Holistic medicine, 47

Human intervention, 46, 56

Human rights, 96

Identity: blindness and, 84–88; collective, 6, 13–14; difference and, 76; of disability, 140, 158; formation of, 5–7, 13–14; and individual suffering, 82–89; normal and abnormal compared, 83–84; social, 5–6, 39, 88, 111

"Identity crossings," 77–78

Ideology: of normalcy, 98; of "person-first," 7, 10–12

Image: cultural, 13–16, 24; difference and, 146–55; and imitation, 143–75; of inability, 155–67; mimesis and, 167–75; of normalcy, 140–41, 148–51; ordinariness standard and, 151–55; society and, 83, 133–36, 144–46

Imaginary, 128, 136–37, 138–40, 154

Imitation and image, 143–75. *See also* Mimesis

Impairment: conceptions of, 66–67; definition of, 51; and disability compared, 52–53; individual approach to, 59; onset of, 78; origin of, 113–18

Implants, cochlear, 63

Inability: political and social issues of, 161–65; possibilities for, 166–67; problem of, 155–67; technology and, 157–60

Inaccessibility. *See* Accessibility

Inclusion: and adaptation, 163; identity formation and, 16; in minority group, 161; obstacles to, 80–81; and ordinariness, 153; privilege of normalcy and, 155; as solution to exclusion, 144–48. *See also* Exclusion; Mainstreaming

Incurable disabilities, 151

Individual suffering, 56, 73–111; adolescent experiences, 73–75; adult experiences, 75–81; facing issues in, 89–93; identity and, 82–89; mercy killing, 103–11; useless difference and, 93–103. *See also* Tracy Latimer case

Industrial Revolution, 1, 155–56

"Infinite plentitude," 128–29

Injustice, political aspects of, 101–2, 111

Institutional discrimination, 52

Integration, 81, 147–48, 165–66. *See also* Inclusion

Interactional sightedness, 74
"Interpersonal commerce," 103
Intervention, human, 46, 56
Interviews: with blind persons, 121–28; in
    Disability Resource Centre, 156–61; with
    parents of disabled children, 121
In Unison, 146–48

Judeo-Christian ethos, 28
Justice, 107; and injustice versus misfor-
    tune, 101–2, 111

Killing, merciful. *See* Tracy Latimer case
Kleinman, Arthur, 61, 67
Knowledge of body, 125

Lacan, Jacques, 128–29, 131–33, 136–40,
    154
Latimer, Laura, 105–6, 108–9
Latimer, Robert. *See* Tracy Latimer case
Learning disabilities, 78
Legislation: accessibility, 129; building
    codes, 131; environmental, 141; rights of
    disabled people, 167–68
Levinas, Emmanuel, 103, 106–7; and the-
    ory of suffering, 96–101. *See also* Other
    (Otherness, Othering)
Lévi-Strauss, Claude, 165, 166
Liminality, 75, 81, 83–84, 169

Macula, 8, 92, 117
Macular degeneration, 117
Magnification technology, electronic, 25
Mainstreaming: Finger's experience with,
    62, 63; identity formation and, 8–9; as ide-
    ology, 66; as reality, 66; rehabilitation and,
    140; and "world of the normal," 68–69
Mairs, Nancy, 70–71, 132
Mannerisms, 137–39
Marginalization, 20, 49; collective, 22; com-
    munity and, 18
ME (myalgic encephalomyelitis), 118
Media, representation in, 12, 24, 68, 107
Medical science, failures of, 22
Medicalization of disability, 53
Medicine, holistic, 47. *See also* Biomedicine
Mercy killing. *See* Tracy Latimer case

Metaphysical questions, 60, 102; acceptance
    and, 25–30; biomedicine and, 30–36;
    mind-body connection and, 35–36
"Metric of suffering," 68
Mimesis, 167–75; belonging and, 173–75;
    disability movement and, 167–68; nor-
    malcy and, 172–73; replication and,
    169–70
Mind-body connection, 35–36
Minimalist orientation, 128–40; to accessi-
    bility, 129–30; the Imaginary and, 138–40;
    and sense of Real, 131–32; societal image
    and, 133–36
Minority groups, 60, 161–62
Misfortune, political aspects of, 101–2, 111
Mortality, 65, 96
Movies, disabled represented in, 12, 24, 68
Multiple realities, 90
Multiple sclerosis, 60, 71, 78, 132
Murder. *See* Tracy Latimer case
Myalgic encephalomyelitis, 118
Mythology, 164–65

Natural body: cultural representations of, 68,
    82, 98–99; identity and, 118, 120–21; risk
    and, 56–58; society's views on, 47–48, 144
"Naturalized humanity," 170
Natural movement, 79
Negative attitudes, 11–12; changing, 81
Nietzsche, Friedrich, 7, 82
Nondisabled persons: attitudes of, 95; inter-
    action with, 11, 100–101
Normal, world of the, 48, 52, 61, 68–69,
    94–96
Normal comparisons: and abnormal compar-
    isons, 23; and pathological comparisons,
    30–31
Normalcy: belongingness and, 174; differ-
    ences and, 91; as home, 38; identity and,
    10, 12, 13, 82–84; ideology of, 98; image
    of, 140–41; as measurement benchmark,
    110; mimesis and, 172–73; passing and,
    74–75; self-identity and, 32; society's
    views on, 47; standard of, 148–51; suffer-
    ing and, 82–84
Normalizing, 68

Object/subject dichotomy, 84
Obstacles to inclusion, 80–81

Oliver, Michael, 51–52, 61

Ophthalmologists: diagnoses by, 117; examinations by, 8, 19, 32–33, 114–16; pediatric, 121

Ophthalmoscope, 114–15

Oppression, 52, 57, 60, 79; social conditions and, 54. *See also* Persecution

Ordinariness: and extraordinariness, 166; standard of, 151–55. *See also* Normalcy

Other (Otherness, Othering), 34; adaptation and, 140; compulsion to be, 173; inability to imagine, 62–64; passing as sighted and, 169, 172; suffering and, 97–100

Pain, physical, 36

Paralysis, experiences with, 27–29, 34–35

Parenthood, choosing, 41–42

Parents of disabled children: and childhood experiences, 121, 135; interviews with, 121

Parisian, Doug, 134–35, 136

Participation in society, 81, 146–48, 174. *See also* Accessibility; Inclusion

Passage, rites of, 74–75, 77

Passing as sighted, 168–70; in adolescence, 21, 23, 25, 64; identity formation and, 9–10; and mainstream, 67; methods for, 27; privilege of normalcy and, 149; suffering and, 74

Pathological/normal dichotomy, 30–31

Pediatric ophthalmologists, 121

Persecution: experiences of, 20–21; history and, 18

"Person-first" ideology, 7, 10–12

Phenomena, supernatural, 5

Physical pain, 36

Pigmentation of eye, 8, 92

Playing at seeing, 121

Polio, personal experiences with, 61–62

Political consciousness, 57

Politics: collective suffering and, 39; of coming out, 70; identity formation and, 6, 15; impairment as, 57; and inability problem, 143–44; individual approach to, 39; and separation between injustice and misfortune, 101–2, 111

Pollution, effects of, 56, 57

Positive attitude, 161–62

Practical ethics, 107, 110–11

Prejudice, 51–52, 92

Public places, exclusion from, 4, 11. *See also* Accessibility

Public transportation, 52, 79

Questions. *See* Metaphysical questions

Race and racism, 60, 92. *See also* Discrimination; Prejudice

Ramps, 173

Randomness, 46

Rationalistic version of disability, 133

Real, sense of the, 128–29, 131–33, 137–40

Realities, multiple, 90

Reclaiming disability, 13–16

Rehabilitation: as adaptation, 31, 33, 140; and "blindisms," 137, 139; coming out and, 69–70; goals of, 152; and "medicalization" of disability, 53, 55; and scientific-rationalistic versions of disability, 133

Relations, social, 144–46

Religion, 35, 165; answers and, 25

Replication, 169–70

Representation of disability: cultural, 1, 13–16, 24, 88; in media, 12, 24, 68, 107; negative, 1, 12–16, 24, 88; societal, 54

Repression, 10

Retina, 92

Retinitis pigmentosa, 117

Rights, human, 96

Rites of passage, 74–75, 77

Rituals, cultural, 74–75, 77–78

Robillard, Albert, 27–29, 31, 34–35, 48

Safety at work, 57

Scientific version of disability, 133

Seeing, 74, 121

Segregated education, 52, 66

Self, staging of, 118–21

Self-blame, 35

Sense of the Real, 128–29, 131–33, 137–40

Senses, human, 84–86

Sensus comunus, 89–91

Sensus privates, 91

Sighted, passing as. *See* Passing as sighted

Sightedness: interactional, 74; playing at, 121

Smokie. *See* Guide dogs

Snellen eye chart, 114, 115
Social class, 60
Social identity, 5–6, 39, 88; ready made, 111
Social model of disability, 51–60, 82; agenda of, 53–56; collective experience and, 60; criticism of, 56–59
Social suffering, 61–71; collective view of, 65–71; individual view of, 61–65
Societal images, 83, 133–36
Society, 17–39, 64, 75, 87; attitudes and emotions concerning, 37–39; barriers in, 52; belonging and, 19–22, 38–39, 128, 173–74; capitalist, 57; community perceptions and, 18; concept of, 37, 54; ethnicity and, 60; exclusion from, 20–21; failures of, 51; identity in, 5–6, 39, 88, 111; image and, 83, 144–46; individual sense of belonging in, 19–22; issues of, 164; metaphysical questions on, 25–36, 60, 102; participation in, 81, 146–48, 174; passing as sighted within, 21–24; place in, 37–39; relationships in, 144–46; and social class, 60; and social environment, 127; and social factors, 60; as source of disability, 141; values of, 18, 21–22, 47
Sociology, 82
Special education, 66, 133, 173
Sports: accessibility and, 130–31; in adolescence, 64; diminishing eyesight and, 19; expectations for, 163; identity formation in, 8; passing as sighted and, 25–26; suffering and, 73
Staging of self, 118–21
Stereotyping, 136
Stiker, Henri-Jacques, 147, 150–51, 153–55, 164–65
Stubbins, Joseph, 21–22
Subject/object dichotomy, 84
Suffering: adolescent and adult experiences compared, 75–76; biomedicine and, 33–34; cultural image and, 15–16; defining a person, 1; denial of, 58; elimination of, 106–7; family and, 106–11; implications of, 50–51; individual, 56, 73–111; metric of, 68; social, 41–71

Supernatural phenomena, 5

Taussig, Michael, 168–71
Technology: and adaptation, 137, 163; assistive, 79–80, 157; and development of self, 121; "disability identity" and, 156–60; electronic magnification, 25; failures of, 22
Telethons, 134
Television, disabled represented on, 12, 24, 68
Testing, genetic, 41
Thomson, Rosemarie Garland, 172–73
Tolstoy, Leo, 19, 25, 34, 60
Toronto, Canada, 1–4, 11
Tracy Latimer case, 103–5; family suffering and, 106–7; implications of, 107–11; justice for disabled and, 107
Tragic/heroic dichotomy, 170–71
Transport systems, 52, 79

Unemployment rates, 147
Union of Physically Impaired People Against Segregation (UPIAS), 51–52
Useless difference, 93–103; as disturbance, 94–97; implications of, 101–3; the Other and, 98–101

Values of contemporary society, 18, 21–22, 47
Victimage, 100
Vision, measurement of, 116

West, Cornel, 128
Western culture, contemporary, 1. See also Culture
"Why me?" question. See Metaphysical questions
Working conditions, unsafe, 57
World Bank, 68

Zola, Irving: on exclusion, 15–16; on possibility of disability, 77; on "world of the normal," 48, 52, 69, 94. See also Normal, world of the